KNOW
WH
TO QUIT

KNOWING
WHEN
TO QUIT

HOW TO STOP FIGHTING
LOSING BATTLES AND
GET ON WITH YOUR LIFE

JACK BARRANGER

Thorsons
An Imprint of HarperCollinsPublishers

Thorsons
An Imprint of HarperCollins*Publishers*
77-85 Fulham Palace Road,
Hammersmith, London W6 8JB

Published by Thorsons 1991
First published by Impact Publishers Inc.,
P.O.Box 1094, San Luis Obispo,
CA 93406, USA, 1988

10 9 8 7 6 5 4 3 2

A catalogue record for this book is
available from the British Library

ISBN 0 7225 2527 3

Printed in Great Britain by
HarperCollinsManufacturing Glasgow

Contents

Contents

Dedication

This book is dedicated to Karen Noark and Christian Brent — two friends whose wisdom and compassion, along with a willingness to listen, moved me toward a deeper understanding that one does not have to stay in order to be a hero.

Introduction

Chapter 1.

Jobs, Relationships, and the Staying Syndrome

Once upon a time a man — let's call him "Ed" — left home to try his luck in Las Vegas. There, he would find his fortune. To finance his quest, he withdrew four thousand dollars from his savings. By the end of the weekend, he figured to have at least twice that.

Just eight dollars in, Ed hit his first jackpot. For an investment of eight dollars, he gained a hundred. "Not bad!" he thought, and was so exhilarated that he failed to realize he had put in another eighty silver dollars before winning again. This time, the jackpot was only fifty dollars. No matter, he was still ahead. Moreover, he enjoyed the attention when he won a jackpot, and enjoyed the sense of community when people wished him luck and hoped that he would win the super jackpot — ten thousand dollars.

The prospect of the ten-thousand-dollar payoff so beguiled Ed that he went through five hundred dollars before winning another jackpot. Yet there was some good news — he did hit the bells for the two-hundred-dollar jackpot. People were patting him on the back now and he enjoyed the camaraderie. Winning felt good, but he failed to notice he had less now than he had come with.

Ed began to feel the loss when he was down a thousand dollars. While he had some momentary concern, he buoyed himself up with one hope: that ten-thousand-dollar jackpot had to be close. He was only a fourth through his money, and three triple bars would have put him on Easy Street.

Fourteen hundred dollars later, just as he began to get really worried, a thousand dollar jackpot convinced him his luck was turning again. He could see the flashing lights and wailing sirens.

Twelve silver dollars later he hit a fifteen-hundred-dollar jackpot. Bells, sirens, and camaraderie pushed him on to a new resolve. Yet Ed was becoming aware of an increasing sense of boredom and told himself, ''There's got to be a better way.''

To overcome his increasing despair, he focused on the ten-thousand-dollar jackpot. He explored ways to spend the money: a down-payment on a good car, paying off the credit cards.... Eight more times he came within one triple bar of winning. This had to be a divine sign. ''I'm close; I know it!''

An amazing number of relationships, marriages and jobs fit the pattern of the Las Vegas slot machine. In a destructive or non-nourishing job, increased salaries and the illusion of increased power are jackpots which cover up the fact you are losing. In relationships, the circumstances can be more manipulative. A partner will give you just enough to keep you coming back. You might be losing, but your partner fails to see that. It takes courage to realize that despite all the wins — real or imagined — you might actually be losing.

Spend $10 to Get $3.50?

The slot machine story helps to explain why so many people remain in bad situations so long. Take a look at how the slot machine works: *Not only is it designed to have you lose but it also will have you win just enough so that you will continue losing*. If it gives back too much, the house will not make a profit. If it gives back too little, you will not continue to play. Thus, the machine must be calibrated perfectly.

Ed refused to face the fact that he had only *one chance in four hundred thousand* to win the big jackpot. People have a hard time understanding jackpots. They have an even harder time understanding the realities of life circumstances which might require quitting.

Slot Machines, Jobs, and Relationships

I've had the opportunity to tell the slot-machine story many times. From 1979 to the present I have lectured widely and presented dozens of workshops on the topic of "Finding Your Mission in Life." After these events, some people have asked to work with me individually. Although they knew I am not a trained therapist, many elected to ask my guidance as they wrestled with key life decisions and struggled to find more fulfilling and meaningful lives.

Ken was one such client. He loved his office job so much that he considered himself a winner. Yet his priorities and those of his office changed, and it was no longer a winning situation. Despite being voted most efficient worker, receiving awards, and getting bonuses, he was enjoying his job less and less. When I described the slot machine analogy, Ken acknowledged that he was losing more than he wanted to admit.

He was paying $10.00 to get back $3.50.

Sue faced the same situation in her marriage. She married Rob five months after meeting him. He was such a charmer. Making all the perfect moves, Rob had Sue believing that she was all that mattered in his life. Two years later, *some* of the charm remained; however, most of it had been replaced by blatant ignorance of her needs. Rob still makes some perfect moves — mainly when they are out with others. Sue matters in his life — as long as she doesn't interfere with other priorities. But she is being frozen out and doesn't like the feeling.

People in doomed marriages and relationships often are influenced by the great changes they see in fictional characters in films and on T.V. It matters little to them that these stories have little to do with reality. But a real-life relationship which took years to build — or for that matter to deteriorate — will not change miraculously overnight. With no inner motivation or effort, there will be no change at all. A person hoping for a miracle in a job situation might have to face the fact that the "miracle" will come only with the courage to move to another job.

Even in potentially impossible circumstances, many people still opt to stay. Not because they are self-destructive or love pain. Not because they harbor latent masochistic tendencies. They stay because they have been conditioned to avoid exploring more nourishing alternatives. They have come to believe that staying — even in nearly impossible circumstances — is far nobler than quitting.

Molders of opinion would have us believe that quitting is a disease. Coaches rebuke players who quit in the middle of a season. Teachers scorn students who quit school. In fact, most people do not look kindly upon a quitter. Nor does the media. Rarely will you see a movie or TV show which glorifies a quitter. In those rare portrayals, the circumstances are bad enough to merit our sympathy.

Author Maxwell Maltz points out, in his book *Psychocybernetics,* that we have been conditioned to react this way. Our parents, our teachers, our spiritual leaders, and the impressive power of the media have led us to believe that quitting is negative.

Quitting is a problem in our society, of course. There are towns in Southern California where divorced people actually outnumber married people. Fewer students elect to remain in school these days. Many churches find both members and leaders quitting in legions.

While these social problems are genuine and need to be addressed, we still have our heads in the sand about an equally serious syndrome — staying.

The Staying Syndrome

If staying ever appears in a medical dictionary, its definition might sound something like this:

Staying is a disease with a variety of symptoms, any of which are difficult to spot on first observation. First is a high concern for security. The person does not want to change environments, no matter what the cost. In fact, the person fears change. Second is an obsessive concern about hurting others by moving, usually coupled with an inability to see self-hurt. Third, the afflicted has a sense of hope not rooted in reality. Fourth, the stayer has a very high concern for comfort. This becomes such a concern that great pain is tolerated to maintain that comfort. Fifth, the afflicted has a difficult time getting in touch with real feelings. Unable to admit unhappiness, the victim hopes for a better future or refers to past pleasantries. Sixth is an irrational fear of being selfish, which comes from belief that pursuing one's own well-being is selfish. Fear of the label "selfish" leads the sufferer to endure more personal pain than is healthy. Finally, hard core stayers will defend failure to quit as a noble act and be particularly harsh to those who dare to suggest that such action is not in one's best interests. The stayer is obsessed with the process of remaining even if remaining is highly destructive to mental and physical health.

Staying can keep you in an environment which neglects your well-being. Yet, staying presents a curious problem. If you start to work free of it, others can get nasty. If you move in a direction which best fits your needs, you might be labeled selfish. Getting free of a job which provides little fulfillment may not be a good enough explanation. You will be asked to supply better reasons — such as poor health, a higher-paying job, or the need to live closer to an ailing family.

If you want to free yourself from a destructive relationship, claiming that each of you has grown in different directions may not suffice. Claiming lack of nourishment or excessive criticism may not impress. To soothe the stayers, you may be pressured to come up with such reasons as repeated infidelity or continuous physical abuse. Even with these explanations, some champion stayers won't be satisfied until your arm is in a sling.

If Johnny quits school, we are conditioned to think that the only reason was that he couldn't cut it. No matter what the background, he is a quitter. Yet many potential entrepreneurs ''stuck out'' college when they might have been happier building a business right away. Many optimists remain in dead-end relationships because they are conditioned to believe that *they* are failures if a relationship ends.

It really doesn't matter whether staying or quitting is good, bad or irrelevant. Only *your unique situation* and *your unique feelings about it* can determine whether you should quit or stay. Only your awareness about the condition comes close to expert opinion for your life.

If it is in your best interests to stay, this book will help you recognize this more clearly. If it is in your best interests to quit, you will also see this more clearly. You will have the tools to make a better decision. You can then move into action in such a way that you will hurt the least number of people.

As you read, you'll discover that *those with the courage to get out of hopeless situations can eventually experience greater joy*. The people who stay because of fear gain only temporary approval and safety. Stayers do not gain the self-esteem which comes from acting in their best interests. They don't get the self-validation which comes from doing what they feel is best (even though it may have some initial cost). While society appears to approve of those who stay in bad situations, it does not in any way nourish them.

In the illusion of T.V. and film, bad situations are almost always conquered. If that didn't happen, people wouldn't watch long enough to merit advertising revenues. The movie *Flashdance* wouldn't have had a prayer if the long-struggling dancer had been turned down by the Pittsburgh ballet school and simply returned to her welding job.

Is Quitting Always Best?

Quitting is not the only alternative, of course. *Knowing When to Quit* is designed to help you determine *your* best alternative. If you see that quitting may be the only way to insure future happiness and sanity, I want to help you understand your options and gain the courage necessary to make such a choice.

Cory was a West Point graduate who, after six months as an officer, realized that he no longer wanted to be in the Army. He had made a mistake. His superior officer urged him to give it six more months in order to be sure. Cory complied. Six months later he felt the same, but now he had the support of his superior officer, who worked hard to get Cory released from his four-year obligation.

For Cory, knowing *when* to quit was most essential.

At mid-life Bill wanted to quit being a doctor. He was burned out and could think of nothing but living on a farm. His wise wife Sally insisted that they spend two weeks on a farm in Pennsylvania. By day ten Bill was out of his mind with boredom. He returned to his practice with a plan which still involved quitting. However, instead of quitting medicine altogether, he began to specialize more in what he enjoyed. Not all quits have to be total.

Nancy was one of those seventeen-year-olds who makes one wonder if God is fair — giving so much beauty, brains, and talent to one person. A cheerleader, Nancy was vivacious, graceful, and stunning. But inside all that beauty was intense anguish. Nancy had had enough of playing the ''popular girl'' game. She wanted more time for herself. Right in the middle of the football season she quit the cheerleading squad. Everybody thought she was crazy. Some thought she might have developed some terrible disease. Others thought she was being a snot. However, only what Nancy thought really mattered. She had carefully surveyed her situation and realized that an immediate quit was the most appropriate move.

As a teacher in Nancy's school, I too experienced an anguishing quitting decision. I discovered early in the year that I had made a mistake by accepting a position there. While the words were never used, every command and directive spelled out to ''keep your light under a bushel.'' For the first time in my life, I realized that it would not be in my best interests to stay the whole school year.

I wanted to leave right away. (Three other teachers had done that — and it was only November!) I also wanted to do what was best for my students. I chose to remain until the end of the semester to wrap up what I had set in motion, and to give the school plenty of time to find another teacher.

You may sense that I'm biased when exploring quitting and staying — especially in presenting my concerns about staying being a potentially serious problem. I want to present a balanced and fair exploration of the issues. However, in my **explorations into the problem, I have seen too many people** hurt by unrealistic and impractical ideas about staying and quitting.

More about this in Chapter 8, but I want to warn you in advance that my interviews with hundreds of people and my personal involvement with their experiences have led me to believe that staying is a far greater problem than many are willing to admit.

This book proposes to provide some much-needed balance.

One final point by way of introduction. In the chapters which follow, I lean heavily on examples from jobs and relationships. I hope you'll consider as well how the principles described here can apply to *other* circumstances in your life. We all get stuck in ruts: habits that keep us smoking or drinking too much; dull routines for everyday schedules; group memberships which have lost their meaning; and other non-productive "staying" patterns.

As you read *Knowing When to Quit*, take a look at what these chapters have to say to you beyond your job or intimate relationship. Maybe you need the fresh air a quit could bring to your life?

<u>Chapter 2.</u>

Knowing When to Quit

You're reading this book because something in your life needs changing — your job, your marriage, your relationship, or some other situation.

If only decisions about such life issues were more clear cut. Why can't all the factors lean heavily toward the pro or the con, instead of being so clouded? Yet, life is complex, and so are its decisions. Still, "complex" doesn't have to mean "confusing." For the most part, complexity makes life interesting and challenging. Confusion, on the other hand, robs you of energy and the very joy of life.

You are aware of some inner rumblings, or you wouldn't be reading this. The material in the following chapters can help you to clarify your true feelings, and to discover your power to make the right decision.

Self-Analysis

The next chapter — "Your Desire to Quit Is Telling You Something" — will help you begin to explore those inner rumblings, and to compare them with popular stereotypes about quitting. Sometimes the only way to win is to quit. You may find, for example, that your desire to quit simply indicates that there is something far better for you.

Chapters 4 through 7 provide an opportunity for healthy self-analysis, with questions centered around the following four areas:

- Can you stay and still be happy?
- Will you hurt yourself by quitting?
- Will you hurt others by quitting?
- Is your environment nourishing or toxic?

Some of these questions represent areas you may not have considered. Other questions will help clarify your unique circumstances so that you can make the best decision about what you need to do.

The more thorough your self-analysis, the more you will gain a sense of your most productive move. For instance, it may not be necessary to leave a job or relationship totally. This is only the extreme of your options.

Social Analysis

Moving from self-analysis, Chapters 8 and 9 shift the focus to your environment.

Chapter 8 — "Why Good People Stay in Bad Situations" — explores the reasons people use to justify remaining in unhappy circumstances. You'll sense the weaknesses of some ideas which, while appearing valid on the surface, lose their power when exposed to reason.

Read each of the reasons for staying. Don't fall into the trap of looking at a title and dismissing it. Full commitment requires full exploration.

Chapter 9 — "Winners Never Quit — And Other Myths" — discusses five myths which need to be debunked. These false notions have become part of our social environment and are popular despite being invalid. Conscious awareness of how some of these myths might influence you decreases their power and increases your own.

Decision

Once you've explored yourself and your environment, you'll want to develop tools for decision making.

Chapter 10 — "Discovering the Message of Crisis" — explains another message within you, and what it may mean to you. If you can understand that crisis could be your greatest friend, you will increase your knowledge and clarity significantly. Many crises signal us that a significant decision needs to be made.

Chapter 11 — "Some Thoughts About Seeking Advice" — states firmly my belief that you are the only expert on you. Your circumstances are unique. So is the frame of reference of anyone you seek for advice. If you need to seek advice, this chapter offers guidelines on how best to profit from it.

Chapter 12 — "The Knowing When to Quit Index" — provides a systematic method for "scoring" your situation, so you can pinpoint your best move. The Index can also serve as a guide to help you review any necessary material before making a decision.

Action

Many folks become unnecessarily anxious about taking action because they fail to realize there are many available options. Six possible alternatives are explored in Chapter 13, "Your Six Choices for Movement." Both the theory and the personal examples will help you determine which option — from quitting immediately to changing the situation — is best for you.

Chapter 14 — "Building the Bridge" — encourages you to reach out to resources in your environment which will help you make the transition to a new life. If you choose to quit your current job or relationship, you'll need to establish new support systems. Begin early, explore thoroughly, and build well.

The very short Chapter 15 — "Leaving the Comfort of the Fire" — places the quitting decision in the context of human history. Our primitive ancestors allowed their wonderful home fires to inhibit their passion to explore. When you fail to quit what is blocking you — no matter how wonderful you or anyone else feels about it — you inhibit a major element of your humanness.

An Appendix provides extra copies of the self-analysis questions presented in Chapters 4, 5, 6, and 7. You may wish to photocopy these questionnaires and complete them often as you consider your quit/stay decision. Repeating them over several weeks could help you see trends in your feelings about your situation. In the Appendix, the question sets are grouped into "Job" and "Relationship" subsets, to give you easy access to those which are appropriate for you.

Summing it Up

Your exploration involves four distinct moves. You have already begun to sense that quitting vs. staying is not a black and white issue. Nor is it an issue in which you should allow yourself to be motivated by fear or the desire for outside approval.

The *Self Analysis* chapters will help you look at yourself, your values, and your needs. Various questions and the way you answer them will help you clarify your priorities and values and how they relate to your decision.

The chapters on *Social Analysis* will help you to understand your environment, how it has affected you in the past, and what you can do about it now.

The *Decision* section will give you tools on how to use what you have read in order to make the most effective decision.

The *Action* chapters will give you what you need once you decide to take action, and will help pave the way to what's next.

By the time you complete this book you will have enhanced your knowledge, clarity and power to make the best move at the best time. You'll know when — or whether — to quit!

An Invitation: Keeping a Journal

Quitting — or even considering a major move — can be a potentially disrupting time. Sometimes remaining seems the most sane decision; other times remaining more resembles enduring agony. Sometimes these two extremes can be felt in the same week. (In marriage and relationships, they can be felt in the same day.)

So that you have some idea of where your thoughts, preferences, and experiences are leading, I encourage you to consider keeping a journal. A journal gives you the opportunity to review something later with a clearer perspective. The actual record of events and feelings in your life gives you much greater recall than trying to reconstruct them from memory. The very act of sitting down and writing helps bring up feelings and insights which may not otherwise emerge.

It doesn't matter whether you call it a journal, a diary, or a logbook. It's for you to help you understand circumstances which you are experiencing. You need be the only one to see it — in fact it'll be more effective if you do keep it confidential.

The value of such a journal will become more evident as you read further into this book. I'll be asking you to explore specific questions about your circumstances; having a journal to refer to might help clarify a tough area. In reviewing your journal, you might find certain feelings intensifying. This also will help clarify your decision.

You could write directly in your journal your answers to the various questions asked in the book. Then, as you review your material, you can sense whether your feelings have diminished or strengthened.

A bit of humility from me at this point might shock you: *I probably haven't thought of everything in this highly fragile area of knowing when — or whether — to quit!* A journal could provide a space for insights which come from within the depths of you, insights which shed wonderful light on a seemingly unsolvable problem, and insights which fill the gap between my words on these pages and your unique situation.

Throughout the book I'll be asking you many questions: questions about yourself, your relationships, and your job. You can use your journal to write down your answers, keep track of your progress, and brainstorm ideas.

The greatest value of such a journal is to get a sense of where you are heading. At first you may feel that your relationship is doomed...or that your job is hopeless. However, as you communicate with those involved, you could gain a different perspective. If you have "logged" your feelings, you can sense where they are moving. This will help bring further revelations.

One person might talk with her partner and find him receptive to further communication. This almost always inspires hope. However, as communication continues, she might sense a lack of the consistent commitment necessary to save the relationship. If feelings are logged, this "wavering" is seen more clearly.

Another person may find himself totally committed to the idea of quitting his job. He logs his strong feelings and then begins communicating with his superiors. They listen and then make suggestions. With each suggestion a little more light is seen at the end of the tunnel. The logged feelings show a lessening of despair. What seemed like a hopeless circumstance now appears to offer more hope.

You will do a lot to help your decision making if you can refer to something concrete. Your journal entries will provide both an anchor and a map for your feelings. You will better be able to sense:

- feelings which are consistently strong
- feelings which are running out of steam
- feelings which are inconsistent, and
- feelings which are becoming more intense,

Most people rely on feelings alone to make a decision. While feelings are often a good foundation for making a choice, they may change for reasons which have little to do with your ongoing situation. A good office party or a wonderful session in bed can temporarily distort feelings about a job or relationship.

With a log of your impressions, feelings, and answers to questions posed in this book, you stand much less chance of being "trapped" by passing impressions.

With a personal log, you can keep track of your own circumstances, check your progress — or lack of it, sense how new issues affect you, and prepare a foundation to work from when you use the *Knowing When to Quit Index* to help reach an "objective" conclusion.

In some of the chapters which follow, I've provided procedures for "scoring" your answers to key questions. Totalling the scores and evaluating results will increase clarity, offering a more "objective" perspective. Yet, please be aware that the scores are only guidelines. Getting a clearer focus on what you actually feel is the top priority.

So now you have a pretty good idea of what's coming. Ready for a bit of self-analysis?

Self-Analysis

Chapter 3.

Your Desire to Quit
Is Telling You Something

The desire to quit is a valid and mature response in some circumstances, although most of us have been taught to believe the opposite. Too often, early conditioning ("Get in there and *try*, kid. Winners don't quit.") helps to create guilt about the idea of quitting and to motivate a person to remain longer than necessary in a non-productive situation.

How do you feel about your present job circumstance? Part of your self-discovery is to recognize early messages which may block you from moving in your own best interests today.

Did you learn as a child to deny your feelings? You could be denying strong feelings about your job which are aching to be heard. Conditioning when we're young carries over to adult situations.

In school, dissent might have resulted in some mild punishment. It might even have meant the loss of peer acceptance. But it never meant loss of potential income or the loss of promotion — risks which are real in adult jobs.

If your father stayed at a job he hated so that you might eat, that will have its effects. If family members and friends praised his devotion to his family, the impact upon you will be even greater. If you admire your father, and his sacrifices, that same experience will likely lead you to value such dedication even today, since conditioning when you were very young became a part of your belief system. Thus you may have learned to value self-denial because it was important to people who loved you. They too had been conditioned and, with no bad intent, they passed it on.

Experiences like these, sadly, lead many people to consider a negative working environment to be typical. *Many actually expect the workplace to be a non-nourishing environment.* Some are pleasantly shocked when they work for an employer who makes worker morale a priority.

A secretary who had been a client of mine was well-accepted by her co-workers as long as she kept her feelings to herself. However, when Missy began sharing her inner rumblings about office procedure, acceptance dwindled. Some claimed that she wasn't loyal. Others bluntly told her she was unprofessional. Interestingly, her boss didn't mind. He appreciated knowing what Missy was feeling.

If your mother and father remained in a turbulent and non-nourishing marriage, that will affect how you approach relationships. If Mom did not share her feelings, that helped deepen your learning. If she covered despair with a facade of happiness, that may have affected you more than you realize.

Another part of your self-discovery will be to explore the messages you are hearing within yourself now. Some of these inner messages will "inspire" you to remain in a dead-end job. This "inspiration" could lead you to think that a hopeless relationship or marriage should be endured because that's the noble thing to do. Some messages will lead you to believe something can be gained by remaining in a hopeless situation. As you become more aware of any submerged feelings, you'll begin to understand which messages fit your current circumstances. And you'll learn to differentiate between those which are truly *your* feelings, and those which come from outside you.

In the rest of this chapter, you will explore some important questions which will help clarify these issues. If your circumstances are good, the following questions will have little impact. If you are mentally locked into a bad situation, the following questions might lead to your discovering what you really feel.

Throughout this book I will be asking you to examine *your feelings* about your situation. At times, you may find it difficult to separate your own feelings from the effects of *social conditioning* — the attitudes of your family, school, church, community, and the larger society. While it is certainly ok to accept the attitudes others hold, it is important that you *recognize* when you do so, and to do so *voluntarily*. At times, your own personal beliefs and attitudes may be in conflict with those of important others in your life. That's ok, too, but it will require a good deal of conviction and courage to act on your own, against the advice of others. That, of course, is what being *true to yourself* is all about.

As you explore these issues, be sure to use your log to record what you're experiencing. A journal of your feelings will be a valuable asset when it's time to make a stay/quit decision!

How Do I Really Feel?

It is most important to discover how you really feel. (You could feel much worse than you are willing to admit!) Those who have "buried" their feelings often find that their real feelings gush forth once genuine exploration begins. Sadly, many stop digging when they realize the strength of their feelings. To lose touch with what you are actually feeling is a great tragedy.

In your self-probing it will help greatly for you to be more specific about what is bothering you. By being specific, you give your efforts a much clearer focus. Feelings have a firmer foundation when focused on specifics. Consider the following groups of statements. Contrast the first statements, which are quite general, with the second, which are much more specific:

General: If I quit that job, I'm going to feel a lot better.

Specific: If I quit that job, I'm going to sleep better nights, and I'll probably get rid of this very nervous stomach.

*   *   *

General: If I break this engagement, I'm going to feel a lot better about myself.

Specific: If I break this engagement, I will escape an extraordinary amount of criticism. I will also be free of my fiancee's trying to manipulate me to be someone I don't want to be.

*   *   *

General: I just don't think that remaining a member of this church is a good idea.

Specific: By remaining in this church, I am constantly pressured to compromise my views on what is a good relationship with God.

Are My Expectations Realistic?

A better question may be, "Can I really expect the situation to be any better somewhere else, or with someone else?" In a bad job, the frustration might come from a superior who's insensitive and overly demanding. With a more sensitive supervisor the job would improve. The expectation to be treated better is realistic if you're willing to move. It may not be realistic if you are stuck on remaining in the same job. If you try three different jobs and find that you can't get along with the supervisor, it's time to look within for the source of the problem.

If you feel that your expectations are realistic, you might want to explore if those expectations would hold up in another job. Sales reps who are quick to complain that they want to make more money often don't want to take the risk of working on a commission-only basis. Most sales managers consider this unrealistic.

An expectation which is both realistic and genuine to you may not be considered so by others. When I decided to return to teaching, I opted to teach high school — hoping to teach seniors on the advanced level. In a tight teaching market that was a highly unrealistic expectation!

Expectations can run rampant in relationships and marriages. The media portray relationships and marriage so unrealistically that we cannot help but be affected. A good question to ask yourself in relationships is "Is what bothers me about my partner something I would have only with *this* partner?"

Am I Willing to Pay the Price of Quitting?

Consider what you might experience in quitting a job, marriage, or relationship. Here are some of the possibilities:

- The criticism of family and friends
- A temporary loss of self-esteem
- A loss of income
- The sense that it was a mistake to quit
- The possibility of hurting other people
- The fear that you are selfish
- The feeling that you quit too soon
- A loss of friends
- The fear that you might not find a better person
- The feeling that you might have been able to save the situation

Let's quickly consider these possibilities.

If the *criticism of family and friends* is a key factor for you, you need to determine just how important their acceptance is to your personal well-being. Ask yourself whether their acceptance is unconditional or manipulative. Do your friends and family accept you as you are even if you make a number of mistakes? Or is their acceptance based upon your doing what they expect? Exploring this aspect can be painful.

A temporary *loss in self-esteem* can best be considered by realizing its potential alternative — a rise in self-esteem. Books are filled with case histories of people who after an initial period of devastation, felt stronger and better about themselves a few weeks after they left their doomed relationship or marriage. Author Richard Nelson Bolles (*What Color Is Your Parachute?*) tells of many who felt both better and stronger after having the courage to leave a non-fulfilling job.

Mike experienced an eventual rise in self-esteem when he left his twelve-year job with an advertising agency:

> *I thought that I was going to feel bad about myself because of the drop in prestige and salary. However, I felt good about myself right after I started the new job. While I wasn't expecting to be treated that well as a new employee, I was pleasantly surprised to see how supportive everyone was. I quickly learned that I didn't have to fake it anymore. I didn't have to lie to people about what to expect. If I just could have had a preview of that good feeling, I would have quit a long time ago.*

Loss of income is a trade-off which is more difficult to discuss. Your own feelings must always be the final determiner. You need to decide if compensating rewards merit your move. Explore the potential for a higher income. If a sales rep has been selling one product for years, a move to selling another product makes an initial loss of income highly probable. However, if the new product is one the rep really believes in, the loss of income will almost certainly be only temporary, and an eventual rise in income is equally likely.

The feeling that it might be *a mistake to quit* must always be weighed against the question, "Is it a greater mistake to stay?"

The fear of *hurting other people* will be discussed in Chapter 5, along with the fear of *being selfish*.

If you fear you might *quit too soon*, give yourself more time for your decision. However, be willing to consider the alternative: you might have already remained in a bad situation too long. The awareness you are gaining will help you clarify both your situation and your feelings about it.

The potential *loss of friends* from a quitting decision may appear overwhelming. I have interviewed many people who told of seemingly solid friendships quickly decaying. The converse to this is that when you finally get into a better environment, you start making new friends. You needn't give up old friends; you simply have more choices.

The fear of *not finding a better person* after leaving a relationship or marriage is common. This fear blocks both movement and clarity of thought. People have told me, "I'll wait until I meet a better person, then I'll move." In non-marriage relationships, this has only a slim chance of working. Within marriage, with its deeper legal and social complications, this is far less probable. No matter what the circumstance, one rule holds: *if you've done all you can and the relationship cannot be saved, get out of it*. At least the relationship you have with yourself will be better.

The fear that *you might have been able to save the relationship* arises more from guilt than reality. While it takes only one person to hurt a marriage or relationship, it always takes two to save it. As people grow in relationships, they find that they no longer want to continue with certain aspects. A partner's obsession for "stepping out" can rarely, if ever, be saved by increased love from the spouse (despite myths to the contrary). One partner's increasing need for security can rarely be solved by the other working harder during a recession. Increased work hours usually only increase tension.

What Will I Gain From Quitting?

When most people think about quitting, they focus on the potential loss. Even those who talk about potential gain many say, "It will feel so good just to be out of that job," or "How wonderful not to have to listen to Harry complain anymore."

How sad that more of us don't focus on gains, rather than on losses. Most of us have been conditioned to be much more specific about the negative. (Watch any TV news show and see how many positive events come up!)

Coming up with a list of the probable gains from getting out of a bad situation demands a good deal of effort. Friends and family are quick to point out what could go wrong, of course, and so will your own thoughts. Thus, it's a good idea to think about as many specific gains as possible. They may not come as easily as specifics about what could go wrong, but a particular effort to identify them will provide the necessary balance for making your decision.

Here are some specific gains which you could experience should you decide to quit your job, relationship or other situation:

- I'll make more money
- My skills will be more appreciated
- I will have more self-esteem for having the courage to take this leap
- I will work with more intelligent people
- I will have two extra hours a day for my family
- I can work at my own pace

- I can meet other people without experiencing jealousy
- I will have more sexual freedom
- I will be able to say what I am feeling without wondering whether I am going to hurt someone
- I will have two extra weeks of vacation a year

What gains are possible for you? Write your ideas in your log.

Am I Rushing This?

Droves of unsolicited advisors will swarm to urge you to "go slowly." Their zeal in bringing this to your attention means you'll need to think carefully about this question before talking with anyone. Those most involved with you will be the most likely to ask this question.

Actually, it's a very good question.

It is also a trap.

It is a good question because you do want to be sure that you are responding to your own needs instead of reacting to external pressures. You were probably taught at an early age to be concerned about being a premature leaper. Not much conditioning urges us to be concerned about *remaining too long* in bad circumstances.

Once you are bold enough to ask if you're moving too fast, other related questions begin to show up:

- At what point have I thought enough about my situation?
- At what point do I know that my circumstances are hopeless?
- At what point is "hanging in there" futile?

It can also be a trap because some will ask, "Are you rushing things?" — not out of genuine interest, but as an attempt to manipulate you. "Wait" may translate into "Let's not face it right now." The suggestion that you might be moving too quickly could be a smoke screen to shift attention away from the real problem. Any time you find that your focus is being shifted away from the problem itself onto the speed at which you're trying to deal with the problem, look closely for the other person's motivation. Is this a potential trap?

Is There Any Light At the End of the Tunnel?

This is *the* question, of course. Whether your concern is about a relationship or a job situation — there just might not be any hope. As long as you have hope, you will not have to face the potential reality of change. However, once you realize that there is no ''light at the end of the tunnel,'' you *know* change is the only solution.

Bob wanted to save his relationship with Marcy. However, Marcy kept raising the ante until it became unbearable for him. At first, Marcy wanted to have a grand piano in their small apartment. Then she wanted to be able to play it any time she wanted. Bob conceded to these demands even though it meant that he had to study at the library in order to prepare for his bar exam.

Bob realized there was no light at the end of the tunnel when Marcy demanded that he be in the apartment when she was practicing. She argued that any man of hers should want to hear her practice; Bob suggested that was ridiculous. Marcy flew into a tantrum, crying that she could only marry a man who was *totally* devoted to her. At this point Bob was *totally* convinced that he should terminate the engagement!

Bob's was a sharply defined revelation. Some come more slowly and are not as clear.

Morgan was the head of a sales team selling women's beauty products. She knew that she was a good manager and liked the high commissions which came from her sales and those of her staff. However, as the size of the sales force grew, so did her problems. She found herself fighting for the right to remain on top.

On a good week Morgan would average $2000 in commission; that took sixty hours. Then a point came when sixty hours work would only bring about $1600. To get back to the $2000 level and remain a manager, she was approaching an eighty-hour week. She began to wonder where she was headed:

> *That's very good money for a woman... for anyone. However, I found that sitting on top of the mountain was increasing in price. As others sold more, they would be promoted and thus their monies would not be credited to me. I also came to the point where keeping up with the competition required more than a hundred hours a week. I had put three years into that company. Yet I realized that if I didn't get out then, I would become hooked on an insane lifestyle.*

Whether there is any light at the end of the tunnel is the crucial question to which all the others lead. The success of your own self-analysis process depends upon how honestly you answer yourself.

Again, a reminder to keep track of your feelings in your journal as you give consideration to these questions.

Chapter 4.

Can You Stay and Still Be Happy?

This alternative must be explored no matter how you feel. If you can stay and be happy, the other questions may be unnecessary. As you focus on the good, you must determine *how much good* is necessary to convince you to stay.

To get yourself started on this exploration, "brainstorm" — in your log — short lists of answers to these questions:

- What would it take to have me stay permanently?
- What would it take to have me stay three months?
- What would it take to have me stay three weeks?
- What would it take for me to continue tomorrow?

Don't worry about how your answers appear. A high priority of brainstorming is putting down exactly what you feel without judging yourself or being concerned if it's a good response. If it would take triple your salary to have you stay in your job, put it down. If it would take an additional ten years of maturity — yours or your partner's — to keep you in a relationship, put it down.

It matters little how consistent you are when making up these lists. At this point you are simply exploring your feelings and establishing priorities. As you move further into self-analysis, you will probably want to revise your lists:

I accepted too little for the three-week plan.
I should have put a promotion in the three-month plan.
When you get right down to it, I don't even want to face Sally tomorrow.

Don't be hard on yourself for changing your mind. If you have buried a lot of your feelings, be thankful they're finally emerging. Don't stifle them: it's possible you've been doing that for a long time.

Sam was a brand new teacher at a prestigious private school. Two weeks into the job he realized that he was cloistered with thirty-five workaholics. In addition to being in charge of a boy's dormitory, Sam had to direct three plays. All this in addition to a full teaching load. Single and twenty-four, Sam realized his social life would be minimal.

Feeling overwhelmed when he sought my help, Sam admitted that he might have made a mistake. We explored four options: quit immediately; make it to the end of the term and quit; get another job at the end of the year; survive two years and improve the chances for getting a better teaching job.

Sam quickly realized that an immediate quit wasn't a good idea. He hadn't given himself enough time to adjust to the job, and he knew first year teachers had it tough. He was new to drama, and that would also take time. The work in the dormitory was something he despised; he felt the boys were undisciplined animals. Yet, he was still curious to see if his view would change with time.

Quitting at the end of the term seemed to be a good possibility. In a few weeks he would have greater clarity.

However, his resume would look better if he remained a year. But would it be that much better?

To have a chance at a *good* teaching job, Sam knew he would have to remain two years, to add credibility to his sparse resume. Staying two years would also give him a clearer view of the teaching profession — and of himself as a teacher.

With options to consider, Sam's morale improved. While he was not happy in his job, he acknowledged that he had not given his situation enough time. He decided to stay for the full year and systematically keep track of how things went for him at school — using the questions you'll find later in this chapter.

Your circumstances and environment are always unique. By brainstorming you can consider various options. You could begin by thinking that staying is a good idea. Then, in the middle of the night some deep-seated feeling might surface. Often, when you put these feelings on paper, other options are seen more clearly.

These new-found feelings could tip your thinking in favor of quitting. Or they might cause you to wait three to six weeks before making a decision. In a couple of days, what seemed so pressing may not seem as important. What is most important is that you *begin* thinking about whether you can stay and be happy.

Some Questions to Ask Yourself About Your Job or Career

The first group of questions relates to careers and jobs. Place an X next to any of the questions to which you could answer yes. Remember that it is not the total or even the interpretation of that total which is most important. What is most important at this point are the feelings which come to you as you answer the questions. Use your log to record your answers — and be sure to *date* your log entry.

_____ 1. Will my physical health be hurt by remaining?

_____ 2. Will my mental health be hurt by remaining?

_____ 3. Am I staying in these circumstances *mainly* because I have invested a lot of time in them?

_____ 4. Is the fear of what lies ahead adversely affecting my decision?

_____ 5. Am I experiencing an unusual lack of personal fulfillment?

_____ 6. Is it possible that I might be stuck (unable to move myself)?

_____ 7. Would I be relieved if I were removed from my situation?

_____ 8. Does my staying strongly indicate that I have become stagnant and/or afraid to move?

_____ 9. Am I remaining because I think I am "too busy" to look for something different?

_____10. Am I unhappy enough in this environment that it could be psychologically harmful?

_____11. Have I come to the point where there is no light at the end of the tunnel?

_____12. Has my situation eroded so slowly that I may not yet be aware how bad things really are?

Before you tally the X's, look at the questions again and note if any significant feelings came up as you were reading each one. You might want to write those feelings down. (Believe me, the feelings that surface when you confront yourself honestly are far more important than any tally of X's.) If these feelings get stronger, that's a good sign that your genuine feelings are beginning to surface.

For those who must have guidelines, what follows is meant only to help you think more deeply about your unique situation. There are no exact scores, and no averages *for you*, so please do not be seduced into a premature decision by the numbers. OK, tote 'em up.

Total _____ (J-1)

A total of 9 - 12 suggests that your circumstances in the workplace could be unusually bad. Quitting should at least be explored.

A total of 6 - 8 suggests that you may not be experiencing enough joy and fulfillment in your work. However, with this total, you might at least feel better about remaining for a time to clarify your situation. The exploration of quitting might be a good idea.

A total of 3 - 5 may merit exploring your situation more thoroughly. Some might consider this many negatives "par for the course" and will be content with so few "conflicts." Others might experience those three to five areas so intensely that they consider their situation unbearable. It is here that your personal priorities must be explored. Many will settle for far less than they deserve. You need to ask yourself whether — despite your total X's — you are willing to put up with more of the same.

Any total under 3 suggests that you might be doing fairly well in your work environment. However, your answers to these questions may not fully represent your feelings about your job. If the feelings persist, trust them. They are much more important than any total.

Some Questions to Ask Yourself About Relationships or Marriage

In the list below, place an X next to any question you answer yes. Note any feelings which emerge as you read the question. Trust those feelings and consider writing them down in your log as you experience them.

_____ 1. Will my physical health be hurt by remaining?

_____ 2. Will my mental health be hurt by remaining?

_____ 3. Am I staying in these circumstances mainly because I have invested a lot of time?

_____ 4. Am I inhibited to a point where I am not free to to be myself?

_____ 5. Do I enjoy being with my partner less and less?

_____ 6. Is my conditioning about relationships or marriage affecting my decision to quit or stay?

_____ 7. Have I been denying any strong feelings which I might have about the relationship?

_____ 8. Is there little chance we can change things for the better?

_____ 9. Have I come to a point where there is no light at the end of the tunnel?

_____ 10. Has my situation eroded so slowly that I may not yet be aware how bad things really are?

_____ 11. Am I limiting myself by believing that there is just one person "meant to be" in my life?

Once again, I want to remind you that the feelings you experience as you consider the questions are far more important than any total. And for those who would be helped by some guidelines, what follows is just as unscientific as the job-related guidelines discussed earlier. The following totals are meant to stimulate thinking and are not meant to represent any "averages."

Because there is only one other partner to work with, your chances for effecting meaningful change in a relationship or marriage may be better than in the workplace. Hence, the scoring will be slightly different from the job-related tally.

Now add your total X's for the questions above.

Total _____ (R-1)

A total of 8 - 11 indicates that your relationship needs a lot of work. (Or perhaps both of you are perfectly matched in your love of conflict!) At least consider that you may be more in love with the *idea* of a relationship than the particular relationship you are in. A total this high indicates you should at least explore quitting the relationship.

A total of 5 - 7 suggests enough inner turmoil to merit looking at your relationship more closely. A 5, 6, or 7 does not usually indicate a terrific relationship, but it does indicate that the possibility of avoiding a quit *depends on how much your partner is willing to change in areas which you deem important.*

A total of 3 or 4 at least suggests that your circumstances *may* not be that devastating. However, two or three of the areas you answered yes to could be insurmountable. Once again, it is your feelings and your priorities which are important — not the raw total. This total might suggest the need to breathe some more harmony into your relationship.

A total of 1 or 2 suggests on the surface that your
relationship is working very well. Yet, be bold enough to face
how strongly you feel about those one or two issues. If you
sense that you will never be free to be yourself, you may have
an insurmountable problem in the relationship.

Remember, at this point you are just exploring. You may
be developing a sense of where you're headed, but don't
make any decisions yet. Continue this process of self-analysis.
Answering the questions in the next three chapters will help
you further clarify your thinking.

Chapter 5.

Will You Hurt Yourself By Quitting?

Take a bold look at how much harm can be done by staying on a toxic job.

You'll have no problem finding advisors to tell you how much you can lose by quitting a job. Most people are stayers who do not want change. Thus, most cannot give you adequate counsel on why staying in a counterproductive job might be doing you more harm than quitting.

The fact that they cannot offer adequate counsel will not, however, stop them from offering advice. Just as the odds are solid that you will not win playing a Las Vegas slot machine, so too are the odds that more people will tell you that you will hurt yourself by quitting. You need more objective help — help which relates to your unique circumstances, your priorities, and your frame of reference.

The questions in this chapter will help you clarify whether you might be hurting yourself by staying or quitting.

Will You Hurt Yourself By Remaining In Your Job or Career?
    The following "survey," like that in the previous chapter, is not a scientifically validated test. It is a tool for exploring your feelings. The numerical guidelines which follow the survey are not meant to freeze you into any category. They are meant to stimulate further thinking.
    Place an X next to any question to which your answer is "yes":

_____ 1. Is this job causing significant harm to my mental or physical health?

_____ 2. Could I could gain more by quitting than staying?

_____ 3. Am I staying mainly because of economic security?

_____ 4. Am I stuck in a job which is doing me more harm than good?

_____ 5. Could I be staying in my work because it's predictable and I don't want to change?

_____ 6. Could I use my talents better in another job or career?

_____ 7. Am I staying because I don't want other people to think I'm selfish?

_____ 8. In the process of making my superiors winners, am I becoming a loser?

_____ 9. Am I afraid to admit to myself that this job is falling far short of my expectations?

_____10. Am I exhausted at the end of every working day?

_____11. Can I say that in relation to my job, the best days are behind me?

_____12. Would I be secretly relieved if I were removed from my job?

Total _____ (J-2)

A total of 9 -12 strongly suggests that staying is going to hurt you. Quitting whatever you are experiencing should at least be strongly explored.

A total of 6 - 8 indicates that staying *might* hurt you. However, with this total, chances are you will at least feel better about remaining in order to clarify your situation.

A total of 3 - 5 suggests that you should at least explore the real cost of staying. Be willing to search for a better alternative if your feelings continue or get stronger.

A total under three suggests that you may not be hurt much by staying. However, if strong feelings persist, probe further to determine what they're revealing.

How Might You Hurt Yourself Staying in a Bad Relationship?

Some people have such an outdated view of relationships or marriage that they think being hurt is typical. Much traditional teaching about relationships leads folks to believe that a high level of sacrifice is essential for a relationship to work.

Meeting your partner "halfway" can be mutually nourishing. It can also be mutually destructive. Thus, it is essential to be willing to see how much you could be hurting yourself by staying in a deteriorating relationship.

In relationships and marriage the focus is mainly on one other person. However, other factors can affect the picture. Fred felt Eileen was the right woman for him, and they were seriously considering marriage. However, Fred had two problems: Eileen's daughters, Sharon and Julie. Fred found out very quickly that he was considered an invader; both girls wanted him out.

What made it all very sticky was the fact that Eileen refused to acknowledge any problem. To Eileen, her daughters were wonderful, and any man who could not see this was not the man for her. Thus, the burden was on Fred. While the problem with the girls seemed nearly impossible, he loved Eileen enough to give it a try.

Fred was not able to express what he was feeling, his level of frustration increased, and he realized that this situation was going to hurt him. He also accepted that leaving Eileen would hurt him. If the girls had made Fred miserable before, they were turning it on now. One night during a particularly tempestuous meal Fred stood up and threw his napkin down on the table. He looked directly at Eileen:

These two girls are yours, so I don't really have the authority to discipline them. But if you want me to stay here, you are going to have to help me keep these spoiled little brats in line. I'm not going to stay here and fight them. I'm afraid they have very little chance for happiness in adulthood, because you sure haven't treated them the same way that life is going to treat them.

Eileen and the girls stared at Fred in shock. Without missing a beat, Fred turned to the girls:

Julie, Sharon — this could be your unlucky day. It could also be your lucky day. It will be your unlucky day should I decide that I've had enough and walk out of here. Your mother is going to be miserable and your relationship with her will be tainted with bitterness. If this is your lucky day, we'll work out something so we can all be happy here. One thing I can guarantee you. No more "Mr. Nice Guy" when you pull all those tantrums and other bits of manipulation. Life is going to change for the better for you, because from now on if you pull any of that stuff, I'm going to kick ass.

Fred had the courage to make this highly volatile speech because he realized that he was going to be hurt no matter what he did. Thus, he moved in a direction of meaningful change. In this case it worked. He decided to take the risk of confrontation because he had explored the areas where he might be hurting himself if he remained in the same circumstances. Once he knew the cost and the potential gain, he could move forward with confidence and power.

For six weeks Fred had a fight on his hands. However, he now had support from Eileen. Gradually the girls began to realize that they enjoyed having an assertive man around. They also realized that Fred loved them.

Those who stay in relationships or marriages because they fear the hurt of separation could be experiencing a greater hurt. If the relationship is beyond repair, staying only increases the despair.

The following questions will help you sharpen your thinking. Place an X in the space next to questions you would answer "yes."

_____1. Am I increasingly happy when I am by myself?

_____2. Could the price that this relationship demands be too high?

_____3. Have I been blocking what I really feel?

_____ 4. Am I afraid to communicate my feelings?

_____ 5. Do I have a hard time being myself when I'm with my partner?

_____ 6. Do I feel less good about myself when I'm around my partner?

_____ 7. Am I staying in this relationship just to protect my partner?

_____ 8. Is it possible that there is no hope for this relationship?

_____ 9. Is my partner expecting too much from me?

_____10. Am I staying in this relationship mainly because I have invested so much of my time and myself in it?

_____11. Is it likely that I have remained in this relationship mainly because I feared what others would think of me if I left it?

Total _____ (R-2)

Remember, you don't have an establishment to deal with here. You have only one partner (and perhaps a nagging mother-in-law or some hostile kids), so the chances for the change you want should be better. However, once again, it is what you felt as you were reading the questions — and not any raw total you get — which is more important. If you wish to refer to the following "scoring" guidelines, remember that the totals are primarily for stimulating your thinking and are not meant to lock you into some "typical" category.

Use your log to write down any feelings you might have had. Note if they get get stronger. Trust what's coming from your gut.

A total of 8 - 11 suggests that remaining may hurt you greatly. Your relationship could need significant changes — which would require a very cooperative partner. You should at least *explore* quitting the relationship.

A total of 5 - 7 indicates that you could be experiencing enough hurt to consider either a quit or an internal change. Once again, this depends upon how cooperative your partner is. A 5, 6, or 7 may not indicate a good relationship, but it does suggest that there is a possibility of avoiding a quit.

A total of 3 or 4 suggests that you experience what most couples experience. Your circumstances and environment are probably not overly toxic. However, you still might want to explore improving that relationship.

With any total less than 3, you are experiencing fairly good circumstances, and there is little indication that you will hurt yourself by staying unless the areas you checked are highly intense or unbearable.

Perhaps you are tempted to avoid thinking seriously about the personal cost to you of your decision. Don't let yourself be intimidated by high sensitivity to "me generation" excesses. Concern for your own welfare is not selfish. In fact, you can care for those you love only to the degree that you nurture yourself. If your decision hurts you, you can be fairly sure it's going to hurt those close to you as well.

Before we go on to explore the effects of your decision on others, however, let me remind you to consider areas of your life other than your job or relationship as you deal with the issues in each chapter. Do you need to re-examine some old non-productive habits, such as eating or drinking in unhealthy ways? Have you been seeing the same therapist for months (years?) and getting nowhere? Do you play bridge every Thursday night just because you've been doing so for years? Are you missing some exciting new vistas by always going to the same spot for vacations?

Chapter 6.

Will You Hurt Others By Quitting?

The desire to avoid hurting other people is one of the most noble reasons for remaining. It can also be one of the most stupid.

Very few people consciously want to hurt other people. Most people have great concern about others. While I see isolated examples of selfishness and insensitivity, I see far more examples of compassion and giving.

Yet, when people make important decisions about quitting and remaining, I see action which borders on self-destruction. This centers mainly on those who hurt themselves in order to avoid hurting others.

To Avoid Hurting Someone Else Is Almost Impossible

This reality is most obvious in marriage and relationships. How convenient it would be if couples simply tired of one another at the same time. How nice it would be if a man and woman *equally* decided there was no more life in their relationship! Such mutual timing does happen, but rarely.

Individual awareness grows at different rates. The security-oriented husband all of a sudden wants a life of adventure. The good hostess wife tires of being a good hostess. Close to the wedding, a fiancee discovers she has not lived enough on her own.

Backstage, in the depths of their minds, these seemingly "selfish" people are struggling. Paul wants a life of adventure, but he has a son and daughter in junior high school. Joanne, the "good hostess" wife, realizes that her need could affect her husband's career. Fiancee Cheryl grows increasingly concerned about how much her needs will hurt her future husband.

In each of the examples, someone is going to be hurt by a quitting decision. Yet, each situation also has just as much potential for disaster if the person *remains*.

To be absolutely sure, let's probe further.

Adventure-seeking Paul suppresses his inner drives and toughs it out. He finds his adventure in an affair with a younger woman (I'm not endorsing this!), which gives him a feeling of being younger.

It does not, however, solve his problem. When he finally confesses his guilt, he gains a whole new set of problems. He now has a wife ready to divorce him, and two confused children. He unjustly blames his wife for being insensitive to his needs. Paul's situation is worse now. If the couple had negotiated a way for him to explore avenues of adventure, the crisis might have been resolved. Perhaps one or both of them could have taken a "Windjammer" cruise. Had they talked it out, he might have realized that his wife did actually understand his need to break out of his mold. With sensitive communication, Paul's thoughts of infidelity might have remained just that.

Joanne, the "good hostess wife," is trapped... or so she thinks. Better communication could have provided her support for easing off the hostess role. She might have discovered that not all corporate wives fully play the hostess role. However, she has suppressed her needs to advance her husband's career.

While slightly intoxicated at a party, she complains that some wives are "just parrots of their husbands," a remark which filters back to the boss. Now some company people are no longer comfortable with Joanne. Some of her husband's power in the company is lost, and his potential for advancement is hurt. A deep wedge is driven between Joanne and her mate.

Cheryl decides to keep her feelings to herself about aborting the wedding. She convinces herself that many single people are unhappy anyway. Because she has unnaturally stifled her real feelings, she gets edgy right before the wedding. With these unexpressed feelings, she is a ticking time-bomb. By communicating honestly with her fiancee, both might have been able to come to an understanding. In this case, however, the momentum of the event overrode Cheryl's real desires.

Two threads tie together these three examples. First, Paul, Joanne and Cheryl had to choose between hurting their loved ones and suppressing their own needs. Second, while it may be virtually impossible to avoid hurting other people, sensitive communication can help alleviate that hurt.

The Value of Communication

I am amazed at how many people tough it out alone when thinking about quitting. Why are they so reluctant to talk it over with friends? A number of possible reasons come to mind:

- One might be ashamed of the feelings.
- Others' opinions might add to one's confusion.
- One may fear exposing the strong emotions which might come up.

- One might feel that his or her resolve will weaken in direct proportion to the expression of that resolve.

A problem gets solved more as a result of a person's willingness to communicate than of the actual communication itself. The words are merely the opening gambit.

Here is what I said to the head of the English department when I began realizing my job was hopeless:

> *Martha, I'm experiencing a lot of frustration in this job. I am teaching kids who are quite visually literate. I have lectured at eight teachers' conferences on visual literacy and right-brain learning, but our curriculum is so left-brained and traditional that I feel I am hiding my light under a bushel.*

Martha was a very understanding person, but she gave an answer which made me realize that I might have to quit:

> *Jack, you are a talented person. You are also highly disruptive to the teaching team. We have spent years putting together this curriculum. You are really going to hurt our program if you insist on teaching with your new ideas.*

Whether I remained or quit, I was going to hurt people. This actually made a painful decision much easier.

Communication brings the best to a situation no matter what the final choice:

An executive's announced decision to quit caused her superiors to huddle and give her what she wanted. They did not want her with the competition. She was able to get results, and it made good sense to keep her happy.

An insurance salesman's announced intention of quitting caused higher ups to realize that it might be a good idea to promote him to district manager. The increased responsibility was what he wanted, and everyone won.

A wife's announced desire for a trial separation caused the husband to realize that he was not willing to pay the necessary price to help keep the marriage together. He was as unhappy as she was. Thus, the dissolution of their marriage was done with much less conflict.

Will You Hurt Others by Quitting Your Job or Career?

Once again, it would be a good idea for you to examine your feelings and consider writing them down. Perhaps something from the previous examples brought up a feeling or insight. The same can happen as you ask yourself each of the following questions:

Place an X in the space next to each question you answer "no." (Note that you're checking NO's this time!)

_____ 1. Will my quitting cause any harmful disruption?

_____ 2. Could I be underrating the harm that I might cause by quitting?

_____ 3. Will my company or place of employment be hurt significantly if I quit?

_____ 4. Is it possible that I'm remaining because I don't want to cause disturbance and hassle to certain people by leaving?

_____ 5. Would there be too many unusual physical disruptions (moving, etc.) to my family or friends?

_____ 6. Would it be too much of a financial adjustment for my family or friends if I quit?

_____ 7. Would my quitting necessitate my moving to another town?

_____ 8. If I am without income for a while, would this greatly hurt those I'm closest to?

_____ 9. Will I cause those closest to me to be embarrassed or humiliated if I quit?

Total. _____ (J-3)

Remember that the following are not rigid categories, but instead guidelines to expand your clarity about your unique situation.

A total of 0 - 2 suggests the chances for hurting others could be very high... if your assessment is accurate. Only communication with those involved can determine that.

A total of 3 or 4 suggests a good possibility of hurting others. However, such a total also begs for verification from those involved. Communication might reveal that those close to you are more concerned for your happiness and just might be willing to pay any temporary price.

A total of 5 or 6 suggests some disruption and potential for hurting others — but not to any great degree. Be willing to consider that some harm could come from remaining in your present circumstances. This total also begs for improved communication, and is in no way an endorsement for quitting.

Nor is a total of 7 or more. If this is an accurate assessment, your decision should cause very little disruption. (The key words are "accurate assessment.") Discussion with those involved could quickly verify this total.

Will Others Be Hurt If You Quit Your Marriage or Relationship?
Of course they will! Only if your temperament is highly violent or if you are psychologically imbalanced would your quitting a marriage or relationship *not* hurt others.

Remember, you are striving for increased clarity about your situation. You want some idea *how much* harm quitting would cause. Writing down your feelings as you consider each of the questions will help.

Place an X next to any question you answer "no." (Note that you're checking NO's this time!)

_____ 1. Will my ending this relationship or marriage cause considerable inconvenience?

_____ 2. Is it possible that my partner might experience unusual emotional damage if I quit the relationship?

_____ 3. Could I be overrating my partner's capacity to make it on his/her own?

_____ 4. Will a quit significantly hurt my family?

_____ 5. Will a quit significantly hurt his/her family?

_____ 6. Would I leave *because* I want to hurt my partner?

_____ 7. Will my leaving cause any significant financial disruption for my partner?

_____ 8. Will my leaving cause unusual physical disruption (packing, moving, etc.) for my partner?

_____ 9. Will my leaving significantly disrupt any plans my partner has?

Total _____ (R-3)

The break-up of a marriage or long-term relationship causes considerable disruption in the lives of most people. The following guidelines stay away from rigid advice and instead suggest ideas intended to enhance clear thinking.

A total of 0 - 2 suggests considerable potential for disruption. However, this particular group of questions also are the easiest to answer yes. At this level it's essential to consult with your partner and others who might be involved.

A total of 3 or 4 suggests some disruption; this amount of disruption could be typical for the end of a relationship or marriage. Communication with your partner will help determine if he or she agrees with your assessment.

A total of 5 or 6 is an indication that your potential for hurting others may be minor. However, since each person and each relationship is unique, it's difficult to determine what is "typical." What you may want to do is determine how strongly you and your partner feel about each of the areas where you could hurt someone by quitting.

If your total is 7 or more, you might want to re-evaluate or communicate further with your partner. This total — if confirmed by your partner — suggests that you have a minimal chance of hurting anyone that much.

Involving Others in Your Decision

The best leader is one who allows other people to think that they came up with an important idea. One manager's style is to declare, "Here's what needs to be done, and here's how we'll do it." That style will have a certain degree of effectiveness. Another manager states, "I have a problem here; how do you recommend that we solve it?" This manager will usually have a much higher degree of success. The key to this success is letting the other person *participate* in the decision-making (not the same as seeking advice.)

People need to feel that their opinions are important. The opportunity to participate creates allies. With allies, any situation — including quitting — is much easier to face.

The paired examples below show styles which are likely to get very different levels of cooperation:

Churchmember A tells his wife that he is no longer happy in the church where they have been worshipping for years. He asks her how she would feel about looking into some other churches.

Churchmember B mentions that he has "had it" with their church. He informs his wife that they will worship at another church next Sunday.

****

Teacher C tells her principal that she is no longer going to serve as director of the cheerleaders and drill team. She tells him to find another sucker for the assignment.

Teacher D mentions that she no longer enjoys advising the cheerleaders and drill team. She asks if she can be of any help in finding a replacement.

A rigid quitting decision can produce enemies among your closest allies. A willingness to let others participate in your quitting decision can make allies out of potential enemies.

The next chapter will guide you in exploring how you feel about your environment.

Keeping up your log, aren't you?

Chapter 7.

Are You in a Nourishing or Toxic Environment?

Some consider Los Angeles one of the most toxic cities in America. If one focuses on freeways and smog (and an occasional freeway shooting), that's true. Yet, I love L.A., and I felt this way long before Randy Newman expressed it in his song.

L.A. is a friendly place. Policemen almost apologize when they give you a ticket. People laugh in the supermarkets. A friendship can begin with a casual conversation in a movie. L.A. is fun.

On the surface an environment can appear to be toxic, then, with deeper exploration it can be found to be nourishing. This is an area you'll find it valuable to explore.

Few feel the need to be told by a boss that they are loved. Nor does the average homemaker need to have a supporting pep talk before starting the laundry. What is nourishing in the workplace may not be appropriate between men and women in relationships.

Yet, certain factors stand out in both. Gratitude is nourishing in one's work or marriage. A sense of being valuable and valued is nourishing, whether within a relationship or a career.

Various people I interviewed told me that they felt energized when they were with someone they loved or were in a meaningful job. This was something they felt within, and words of support or gratitude were not essential to the experience.

While some are nourished by verbal praise, others sense acceptance and nourishment simply from the attitude of partners, bosses, or co-workers. (In California, we call this "good vibes.")

One person interviewed said, "I know I'm in a nourishing environment when I can be totally myself, and others not only enjoy this but even feel good because of it. I don't have to worry about how I'm coming across. Whatever I do is more than okay; it is stimulating to them — and thus nourishing to me."

The reverse of this is a toxic environment. While one is not literally poisoned by a toxic environment, it can feel very much that way. In a toxic situation, one's energy is depleted, even sapped. Many in toxic environments feel that they have to protect themselves... or at least not reveal parts of themselves which might upset other people.

If an abundance of gratitude characterizes a nourishing environment, lack of gratitude, along with excessive criticism, describes a toxic environment. One is actually de-energized and may need more rest and recreation to restore lost energy. A nourishing environment promotes the proper digestion of food; a toxic environment inhibits it.

As nourishing environments help people to feel valued, toxic environments tempt people to question their worth. This can happen in a company where excessive loyalty and hard work are expected rather than encouraged. It can happen in a relationship or marriage where one partner tells the other, "You are falling far short of what I expected from you."

I have often walked by a classroom full of students sitting expectantly, waiting for their teacher. They waited because they knew their opinions would be valued in that class. They knew that when they made mistakes the focus would be on the mistakes and not on the persons making them. They sensed that their teacher liked them, and really enjoyed teaching the subject. This is a nourishing environment, in which students enjoy themselves and learn.

The room next door was often totally different. A couple of students express their hope that the teacher would be sick. No expectancy here — just dread. The teacher did not ask for opinions because he considered the students stupid, lacking cohesive thought, or perhaps inane. This teacher's "mission in life" was to make his students aware of how incomplete they were without the knowledge he was about to impart. Such a toxic environment de-energizes even the most frenetic of them.

How nourishing is your job or relationship environment? How toxic is your job or relationship environment? The questions below will help you to assess your situation.

How Nourishing Is Your Job?

For you to remain in your job, you should demand that it at least be a nourishing environment. The following statements describe some features of a nourishing job. Remember to write down in your log any strong feelings which come up as you go through the list. Place an X next to those which apply.

_____ 1. You enjoy being with most of your co-cworkers.

_____ 2. You have the opportunity to use most of your training and talents.

_____ 3. You have the freedom to express what you are feeling.

_____ 4. You have praise and support from your superiors.

_____ 5. You feel that you are contributing something worthwhile.

_____ 6. The people around you give you the idea that what you are doing really matters.

Now add up both the X's and the blanks, and put the totals here:

Total X's _____ (N-J)   Total blanks _____ (J-4)

Incidentally, if these conditions sound too idealistic to you, you might be accepting less than you deserve. You might be caught in the "Las Vegas slot machine" mentality discussed at the beginning of the book ($10.00 to get $3.50).

If you checked 5 or 6, you are very fortunate and might have a hard time finding something as good if you made a move.

If you checked 3 or 4, this is could be "typical," but you need to check the strength of your feelings about what you are missing.

If you checked 2 or fewer, consider that you might not be in a healthy job environment. Check to see how many you checked in the toxic portion and note if there is a significant contrast.

How Toxic Is Your Job?

Toxic means poisonous. A coal town where I lived in Pennsylvania prides itself on its clean air. Yet, as you walk through a supermarket or walk down the streets, you can cut the toxic mental atmosphere with a knife. Ask where the peanut butter is in a supermarket, and an answer is snarled back. Joke with the check-out person, and you are told to mind your own business. The air, streets, and parks are clean. However, it is a very toxic mental environment.

The following descriptions will help you to determine if you are working in a toxic mental environment. Note any feelings as you explore the statements, and place an X next to any which apply to your job situation:

_____ 1. You experience more criticism than praise.

_____ 2. When people talk in groups, you hear mostly complaints.

_____ 3. You are constantly told that you are not doing enough.

_____ 4. You have bad relationships with many of your co-workers.

_____ 5. You are constantly told that you need to do better work.

_____ 6. You do not like what you are doing.

Now add up the number of toxic job environment questions you checked, and write down the total:

Total X's _____ (J-5)

If you checked 5 or 6, both your mental and physical health could be affected adversely. Quitting should be explored.

If you checked 3 or 4, you could still be adversely affected. However, you may want to let other parts of this self-analysis help you with your decision.

If you checked 2 or fewer, your environment may be in fairly good shape, as far as lacking toxic qualities. However, this doesn't automatically insure a nourishing environment.

Check to see if you have a significantly higher total for the
"nourishing" job survey (N-J).

If you have low totals for both the nourishing and toxic
parts, you might be in a boring environment and might want
to explore something a little more challenging.

(Should your totals be about equal on the "nourishing"
(N-J) and "toxic" (J-5) surveys, you may wish to use the more
detailed scoring method at the end of the chapter.)

How Nourishing Is Your Relationship or Marriage?

Relationships and marriage have a far greater potential
for nourishment than do jobs, and nourishment should be at
the top of any relationship's priority list. It virtually feeds and
enhances all other priorities. So little effort can yield so much
good. As nourishment fades, minor problems become more
difficult to deal with.

I am surprised at how many people fail to think about
nourishment when they find their relationship in crisis. Other
qualities are automatically expected — commitment,
dedication, and loyalty — but somehow the element that
makes it all worthwhile is overlooked.

How much nourishment do you need in your marriage or
relationship? Don't assume you're being nourished just
because your environment lacks conflict. A lack of conflict is
simply a lack of conflict.

As you look through the following questions, consider
whether you are experiencing what is being described. If not,
ask yourself if you think the two of you are capable of
experiencing it. Boldly explore any feelings which surface as
you consider these questions. Place an X next to each
question you can honestly answer "yes."

_____ 1. Does your partner openly express appreciation for
what you contribute to the relationship?

_____ 2. Are you told verbally that you are loved?

_____ 3. Do you sense that your partner enjoys being with you?

_____ 4. Do you basically feel good about being around your partner?

_____ 5. Does your partner convey the feeling that you are a positive influence in his or her life?

_____ 6. Do you feel there is a realistic balance between the efforts you are putting into the relationship and the rewards you are experiencing?

Add up both the X's and the blanks, and write the totals here:

Total X's _____ (N-R)   Total blanks _____ (R-4)

If you checked "yes" to 5 or more of the above, you appear to be experiencing a high amount of nourishment. If you are considering quitting the relationship, it should not be because of a lack of nourishment.

A total of 3 or 4 suggests a fair amount of nourishment. What will help most in your quitting decision is to compare this total with your total on the *toxic* criteria which follow.

If you checked 2 or fewer, this suggests low nourishment — perhaps an unhealthy amount. Some will settle for this low level to preserve order or a prestigious relationship. It's a high price.

In workshops and individual conversations, I have experienced some interesting reactions to the six questions above. Some people realized they were in a fairly nourishing relationship and worked with renewed vigor to make it better. Others realized that they had more problems than previously realized and accepted the need to expand communication with their partners. Still others realized they hadn't thought much about nourishment.

How Toxic Is Your Relationship?

While many people will tolerate situations which lack nourishment, those who continue to endure *toxic* relationships often lack the courage or self-esteem to get themselves out. In a toxic relationship you are being mentally and emotionally poisoned. While a non-nourishing relationship is barren, a toxic relationship is unhealthy.

Many people don't even realize that they are in toxic relationships. While friends and family recognize the symptoms, those involved tend to be unaware of — or perhaps to ignore — them. As you read through the following questions, "listen" for any feelings which are aching to be heard. Place an X next to any question you answer "yes."

_____ 1. Does your partner frequently criticize you?

_____ 2. Do you find more emphasis placed on your mistakes than your accomplishments?

_____ 3. Do you feel you have to make an excessive effort in order to get praise?

_____ 4. Does your partner frequently yell at you?

_____ 5. Does your partner criticize you in front of others?

_____ 6. Does your partner often lose his or her temper?

Total _____ (R-5)

A total of 5 or 6 strongly suggests an unhealthy environment. Remaining in such a relationship could indicate an obsessive need for security or terribly low self-esteem. This environment begs for a quit.

A total of 3 or 4 does not yet indicate a healthy environment, however, you need to see if you are getting a correspondingly high level of *nourishment* by checking your total on the nourishment questions. If not, this environment could be destructive for you.

A total of 2 or below suggests no real problems for you in this area. You hope to have a significantly higher total for nourishment — at least a 3. If not, at least consider that you might be in a barren relationship — one that might need some life breathed into it.

I have gone over this list with some clients and students and watched them stare in shock as they realized how much they have endured. For many, this was the first time they had accepted they were in toxic environments. Their relationships eroded so slowly that they failed to sense what was happening.

They coped. They ignored. They adjusted.

When they finally realized the devastating price for their adjustment, long-suppressed emotions gushed forth. If you are experiencing a strong emotional reaction to new awareness of your situation, I urge you to talk with a professional counselor — or at least a trusted friend — so that the unloading can continue. Resist the temptation to keep all of it locked up inside of you. Allowing yourself full expression of these feelings will help you to focus your energies on change and self-renewal. Bottling up the emotions will cost you much in wasted energy (to hold them in) and lost opportunity (to gain insight and to work on making your life better).

Toward Greater Detail

If your "nourishing/toxic" totals were very close, or if you want to probe a little bit deeper in this area, here's a way that you can more sharply define your results. Once again, the purpose of this is to get you to think more deeply about your unique situation — not to get you locked into some rigid scoring.

Ralph scored 3 for the "nourishing" job survey (N-J) and 3 for the "toxic" (J-5). He worked for a highly neurotic entrepreneur and was confused about what to do next. I asked Ralph to tell me, for each of the three "nourishing" items he checked, which of the statements below would apply:

____ This is extremely important to me. (Score 5)

____ This is very important to me. (Score 4)

____ This is somewhat important to me. (Score 3)

____ This is mildly important to me. (Score 2)

____ I can take this or leave it. (Score 1)

Below are the three items Ralph checked for the "nourishing" portion and the scores he gave to each:

2. You have the opportunity to use most of your training and talents. (Ralph chose, "This is very important to me," giving him a score of 4.)

5. You have the feeling that you are contributing something worthwhile. (Ralph chose, "This is somewhat important to me," giving him a score of 3.)

6. The people around you give you the idea that what you are doing really matters. (Ralph chose, "This is mildly important to me," giving him a score of 2.)

Thus, for the items Ralph checked in the "nourishing" portion, his scores totalled 9.

Next I asked Ralph to do the same with the three items checked in the "toxic" portion. However, this time he used the following statements and their corresponding scores:

____ I find this extremely painful/stressful. (Score 5)

____ I find this very painful/stressful. (Score 4)

____ I find this somewhat painful/stressful. (Score 3)

____ I find this mildly painful/stressful. (Score 2)

____ I can take this or leave it. (Score 1)

Below are the three items Ralph checked for the "toxic" portion and the scores he gave to each:

1. You experience more criticism than praise. (Ralph chose, "I find this very painful," giving him a score of 4.)

3. You are constantly told that you are not doing enough. (Ralph chose, "I find this extremely stressful," giving him a score of 5.)

5. You are constantly told that you need to do better. (Ralph chose, "I find this extremely stressful," giving him another total of 5.)

While the nourishing/toxic totals were 3 to 3 on the one level, with the more detailed scoring they were now weighted 14 to 9 in the "toxic" direction. Ralph realized that the toxic aspects — in his unique circumstances — had more impact for him than the nourishing aspects.

You can conduct the same detailed analysis Ralph did. Whether related to your job, your relationship, or your marriage, you can gain greater clarity from this more detailed version of "scoring."

If you wish to analyze your relationship or job situation in detail, apply the "important" and "stressful" scales to assess how *strongly* you feel about each item you checked on the nourishing and toxic question sets earlier in this chapter.

For each question you checked "yes" on the "nourishing" part, use the following:

____This is extremely important to me. (Score 5)

____This is very important to me. (Score 4)

____This is somewhat important to me. (Score 3)

____This is mildly important to me. (Score 2)

____I can take this or leave it. (Score 1)

Add up your scores and write the sum here:

Nourishing detail score _____

Now, for the "toxic" portion use the following statements to assess how you feel about each question you checked:

____I find this extremely painful/stressful. (Score 5)

____I find this very painful/stressful. (Score 4)

____I find this somewhat painful/stressful. (Score 3)

____I find this mildly painful (stressful). (Score 2)

____I can take this or leave it. (Score 1)

Add up your scores and write the sum here:

Toxic detail score _____

Finally, subtract the smaller of the two scores from the larger, and write that figure here:

Nourishing/Toxic difference _____

A difference between these sums of only one or two is an indication that other chapters in this self-analysis section (4, 5, 6) offer more important stay/quit guidelines for you.

A difference of three or more could be significant. (Ralph had a difference of five, with 14 for "toxic" and 9 for "nourishing.") This much difference in either direction suggests your environment may be nourishing enough to merit remaining, or toxic enough to merit quitting.

If you are still confused, you might want to repeat this analysis and scoring every few days to determine where your circumstances (and your feelings about them) are heading. If there is light at the end of the tunnel, the total will move more in the direction of the nourishing. If your circumstances are deteriorating, the totals will move more toward the toxic.

Remember to record the totals in your log each time you reassess your results. The totals you've recorded for the question sets in chapters 4, 5, 6, and 7 will be used later (in Chapter 12) to help you arrive at a well-considered decision about quitting.

****

Now that you have looked at yourself and your feelings, you are ready to look more deeply at other aspects of your environment.

Social Analysis

Chapter 8.

Why Good People Stay
in Bad Situations

There are hundreds — perhaps thousands — of individual reasons for staying in jobs and relationships which are not in one's best interests. We humans are amazingly creative when it comes to dreaming up reasons, excuses, and rationalizations for our craziness! In this chapter, we'll take a look at some of the more common ones. Maybe you'll find yourself here!

STAYING REASON NUMBER ONE:
  "I'm Not Aware of What's Happening to Me"
  How often have you felt a slight pain in a tooth? Because you didn't want to face what it might mean, you probably ignored it. A few weeks later the pain got stronger. Instead of going to the dentist, you took aspirin and hoped for the best. Eventually the pain got to the point where only a stronger pain killer helped. Then, the stronger pain killer failed. Finally, you opted for that last resort — the dentist. When the dentist came back with the X-ray, he shook his head in disbelief and asked, "Why didn't you come in sooner?"

Dentists experience that frustration every day. They cannot understand why so many people wait until the pain becomes unbearable before they will do something to help their teeth.

The same pattern of behavior exists in relation to jobs and relationships. Many wait until it really begins to hurt before thinking about a move. Many of the people I interviewed said they didn't realize how bad their circumstances were because they deteriorated gradually instead of erupting quickly. When circumstances deteriorate gradually, many do not sense what is happening.

June was amazed when she looked back upon her marriage. All of the symptoms were there, but she just didn't want to face them. When Bill began drinking more, he said it helped him relax. Then, he hit her during an argument. That had never happened before.

Bill was so full of remorse that she let it pass. But the hitting did not stop, while Bill's feeling of remorse did. Now Bill began to feel justified in hitting June when she got out of line. Bill's language deteriorated also, and June was jolted to reality one night when he called her an "ungrateful bitch."

When June confronted Bill, he said this was typical for a marriage in its seventh year. He told her that she was going to ruin the marriage if she kept focusing on the negative. When June pressed, Bill went downstairs and had a few drinks.

June began to realize how little she had thought about her marriage situation. For a couple of years now, Bill had been taking a drink or two every night before going to bed. She also realized that Bill no longer talked to her about his job, and she remembered that horrible first time that Bill did not apologize after he hit her.

June was able to confront her husband with the reality: a lack of sensitivity to her needs would mean the end of the marriage. Bill got the message that he had a problem and agreed to seek professional help. In therapy, Bill admitted that his job had also deteriorated. He began to deal with his own problems more effectively, and to acknowledge his need for an alchohol treatment program. Marriage counseling focused on communication and mutual respect.

Few people will work as hard as June to save a relationship. Once she became aware of just how badly her marriage had deteriorated, she set out to improve things. Whether the result is making things better and staying, or deciding to quit, *awareness* of what's going on is the first step.

STAYING REASON NUMBER TWO:
"Everything is Basically Okay"

To act as if things are much better than they really are seems to be the American way. Nevertheless, in a genuine crisis, it is essential to be honest with yourself and those around you. No one is served by "gold-plating" what you are feeling.

Many people remain in a bad environment because they are not aware of their real feelings about it. That gold-plated exterior becomes an act. The problem with most acts is that they become convincing — *even to the actors*. One who is not happy in a relationship may not want the loved one to know.

Many of my friends and close associates are therapists. They tell me that the breakthrough for clients comes when they uncover their true feelings. For many, it is like opening a sluice gate. Once a few buried feelings emerge, deeper feelings begin to surface. (If this happens while you read this book or answer the questions, let it happen. Find a qualified therapist if you need help dealing with strange or frightening emotions.)

A buyer for a major department store, Judy made very good money. While she wasn't fulfilled in the job, she figured this was par for the course. Because she had to visit a number of people every day, it was essential for her to put up a good front. She quickly learned that a radiant smile and a "super positive attitude" translated into higher income. This facade, however, became such a part of her act that she thought it was real, until her true feelings emerged:

> *Of all the places I would not have expected, my gut feelings surfaced at a party with a man that I hardly knew. This guy was really something. He was one of those guys who didn't try to get me in the sack within ten minutes after meeting me. I trusted him immediately. I remember vividly how he looked at me with those sensitive eyes and asked, 'Judy, how do you really feel about your job?' That did it. It was like popping the cork of the champagne bottle. I just began pouring out my feelings like I had to get them out in a set time period. I don't swear that much, but I couldn't believe how many times I used the word 'asshole.' My district supervisor was an insensitive asshole. The people I had to sell to were assholes lacking vision. Finally, I saw myself as an asshole for not knowing how I really felt about my job.*

Judy is not alone. Many play the game very well. Conditioned to hide their true feelings, they need stronger stimuli to shake them loose. This realization could come in the form of anger, but often happens in the form of depression. In fact, one commonly accepted interpretation of depression is as a message from deep within, trying to say that something is not working in your life.

Exploring your own deep feelings — as honestly as you can — will help expose a possible "everything is okay" cover-up in your life. The self-analysis questions in Chapters 4 through 7 will help, but don't hesitate to seek professional guidance if you need it.

STAYING REASON NUMBER THREE:
"Something's Wrong, But I'm Too Busy to Do Anything About It"

In my research on the subject of quitting, I am amazed how many people use "I'm too busy" as an excuse.

As soon as I get some time, I'm going to sit down and explore this more thoroughly.

If I just had more time, I could look for another job.

If Ginny didn't take so much of my free time, I would have more time to see if I wouldn't be happier with someone else.

These are all totally self-defeating statements. Deeply rooted in the staying problem, each makes about as much sense as saying, "I would have gone to a therapist a long time ago if I hadn't been so depressed."

Belena found that she was using this excuse for both her marriage and her work. At work she told her friends that her relationship was exhausting her and affecting her work. At home she told her husband that her job was driving her crazy and that a better job would probably improve the marriage.

As tactfully as I could, I told Belena I was not trained to help her and suggested professional counseling so that she could uncover what was really bothering her.

Belena's mother had lived in perpetual crisis, "too busy" to live life in a fulfilling and meaningful manner. In therapy, Belena realized that she had bought into this mentality and worked to get beyond it so that she could find out what she really wanted to do and make time for it.

I noticed something else in my research. Those who are truly happy in their jobs always have the time to do what they enjoy (even if they are working twelve hours a day). Those who are miserable in their jobs say they're too busy even if they are working only four to six hours a day. To a miserable person, the job appears to be all-consuming. This is what Belena discovered as she crystalized her priorities and managed her time better.

Our society has largely accepted the idea that our work robs us of free time, much needed recreation, and the time to be with family and friends. But, those tempted to use this excuse for marriage or relationships have an even weaker excuse.

If you have the same problem in a personal relationship, you need to rethink the value of that relationship. When conflicts of time exist, the relationship usually gets the short end. While it may be a part of our cultural conditioning to sacrifice family and love interests to further a career, that does not make it any less painful or counter-productive. Conditioning or not, it is still you who establishes the priorities and makes the choices. It is you who reaps what you sow, no matter how proper or important you thought your chosen option was.

If you are too busy to explore better alternatives, then you are too busy to experience a more fulfilling life.

STAYING REASON NUMBER FOUR:
"That's Just the Way Things Are"
Author/lecturer Zig Ziglar offers a valuable comparison among planes, houses, ships, and people. A plane will rust out much more quickly if it stays on the ground. A ship will be destroyed more by the barnacles in the harbor than by the waves pounding it in a stormy sea. A house will become useless more quickly if people do not live in it.

Human beings, too, are much more likely to deteriorate from stagnation than from overuse.

John had been with the same company for ten years. For the past five years he openly admitted that he was not happy with his job. His wife and children were not the problem.

They let John know that they were ready to move and, if necessary, live on a much lower income.

John's family wanted him to have a chance to regain the spark he once had. But John was stuck. He dreamed of a better job. Yet, when it came time to make a move, he found that he couldn't. Something else always had to be done first.

John was stagnating. He couldn't seem to get himself moving in a more fulfilling direction. He had the talent but lacked the drive.

For some people, it takes a symbolic "earthquake" to move them from a stagnating environment into a better one. (That earthquake will later be discussed in Chapter 10 as a genuine crisis.) Others have compared the process to getting a transfusion of new blood.

"I couldn't believe it," said one deserted woman. "When my husband left me and the kids, I thought my life was over. It took me a long time to adjust. However, adjust is exactly what I did. For the first time in my life, I saw new opportunities. I found that I liked running my own life. Before, I cooked three meals a day at exactly the same time, picked my husband up at the same train every day. I would still be doing that if Phil hadn't left me."

If you're stuck in "That's the way things are," you'll read this book, perhaps find it an interesting experience, and then continue life exactly the same as before. It does not matter if you are in a job which offers no promise for the future. It really doesn't matter if the situation promises to get worse. You have adjusted to your rut. That "adjustment" is more important to you than fulfillment.

Stagnant people are the hardest to wake up. Their knee-jerk response is to turn over and go back to sleep.

STAYING REASON NUMBER FIVE:
"I've Got a Lot Invested in Time and Training"
On the surface your investment looks like a valid reason

for remaining in a bad job, relationship, or other energy-draining environment. I have seen teachers totally miserable with their jobs; yet they would not leave because they had invested so much in time and training. That they no longer liked teaching (or their students) was irrelevant.

Happiness in a job, relationship or marriage is totally relevant!

During the ten years I spent as a college teacher, a number of unhappy housewives were my students. Something within pushed them to expand their horizons and go to college. In the majority of situations, the husbands were supportive or at least neutral. In one out of three, however, the wife's increased horizons became a threat.

Joyce, whom I knew both as a neighbor and a student, was in her middle thirties. She hungered to go beyond "just" being a housewife. She wanted to find some fulfilling work and came to the college to begin a thorough career exploration program. Her enthusiasm increased and she enrolled in a number of classes, including my freshman English class. After we joked about my fear that having her as a student might ruin our friendship, Joyce got unusually serious:

> *I'm really afraid of Harold. He has really been nasty this last week. He has made it very plain to me that when he married me, he expected me to be a housewife and a mother. The idea of doing anything beyond that really threatens him.*

Three weeks later Joyce dropped out of the program. After further talks with Harold, she was convinced that she should concentrate on being a wife and mother, and not go into anything else. At least that would keep the marriage stable.

I advised her that she didn't have to give up being a mother and a wife. She could add new dimensions to those roles. However, she never came back to the college, and the staying syndrome claimed another.

I have seen so many people remain in excruciatingly painful relationships because they had invested so much time in that relationship. I have seen students remain in misery by going on to a four-year college after being completely miserable in a two-year college. I vividly remember a conversation I had with one of my students:

JB: "If you are so miserable, why are you going for more of the same?"

S: "I don't want to waste the last two years."

Even at the college level the idea of staying is deeply entrenched.

The staying syndrome often blocks our vision of options. Joan could have worked for a year after receiving a delayed admission. She could have explored other majors or other ways to use her chosen major. She could have told her upwardly mobile parents how she really felt about college, and they could have helped her explore alternative forms of higher education.

I made further efforts to get Joan to do some self-probing:

JB: "Joan, why are you going to continue in a situation which you you hate with a passion?"

S: "I want to be somebody."

JB: "Do you want to be a happy somebody?"

S: "I don't know what you mean."

Case closed.

One of the most courageous questions you can ask yourself is: "Am I remaining in my situation mainly because I have invested a lot of time or training in that situation?"

You may be able to see friends who remain in what you consider to be a bad relationship because they have invested so much time in it. Is it possible that you have some friends who have accrued so much senority or spent so much time in the job that it is difficult for them to consider moving to something better — even if the job is far from fulfilling or nourishing?

For right now forget about focusing on your friends. Be bold enough to consider that you might be caught in this trap yourself. No matter what the investment in time or training, it is never a valid reason for remaining in circumstances where you are no longer happy.

STAYING REASON NUMBER SIX:
"Quitting Would Mean That I Was a Failure"

Look at it the other way. Would you consider that *staying* meant that you were a failure?

We are conditioned to believe otherwise. Who is the more successful — the person who is unhappy but doesn't make any waves or the person who searches for fulfillment in life and boldly keeps seeking until it is found?

That is one of the greatest tragedies of the staying syndrome. People vicariously root for those on T.V. and in books who strike out in different directions. They might cheer when the parish priest announces that he isn't going to take any more and walks away from the church. They might feel good when the ulcer-ridden executive boldly asserts that he has had enough and walks out into the sunset, backed by heart-swelling music. Throats tighten as the mentally abused housewife stands before her insensitive husband and announces that the marriage is over. All of these are just fine — as long as it isn't your parish priest, your father, or your wife.

Many believe that getting out of a bad job, a bad relationship, a failed marriage or a bad situation is a manifestation of failure. This belief works because we allow it to work.

Theresa had been engaged for almost two years to a boy who was much loved by her family. For the previous six months Theresa had wanted to break the engagement, but her mother saw it differently:

Theresa, all of your life you have done things which cause your father and me to feel that you are a failure. Now, it is not that we are saying that you are a failure. But if you run away from this commitment, people are going to get that impression. You almost flunked out of college, and you have only been in your present job for about six months. For God's sake, don't mess up your life by failing to go through with this marriage. I love you so much and want to see you make something of your life.

(Those of you who have just experienced visions of venting hostility on Mom will have to line up behind me.)

Sadly, Theresa didn't understand the staying syndrome. She would have seen how it distorted her own thinking and how it eventually caused her to accept an unhappy marriage. Any attempt to talk to her mother about what she was feeling would only produce a re-run of the same staying tape.

While you might have more fun thinking about a conversation you would like to have with Theresa's mother, it would be far more productive for you to explore the possibility that you may be stuck in the "quitting means I'm a failure" mentality.

Words often are not even necessary. Often it is a feeling which shuts off any inner dialogue. Yet, if you are being influenced — even to a small degree — by this mentality, then inner dialogue and some courageous inner exploration is exactly what you need.

The question you want to ask yourself is this: Is it possible that I am remaining in counter-productive circumstances mainly because I fear that quitting those circumstances would cause me to feel that I'm a failure?

Then you could add another question: Is it possible that I would be a bigger winner if I got out of those counter-productive circumstances?

STAYING REASON NUMBER SEVEN:
"I'm Afraid Anything Else Might Be Worse"

The fear of change is a powerful force for keeping people in counter-productive situations. Too many will accept depression and lack of nourishment because they fear moving on to something else.

A good friend of mine was offered an administrative job in a school in Hawaii. When he was discussing it with me, Ken made up reason after reason for not taking the job. He wanted me to agree with his reasoning. (He recognized that he was dealing with a friend who was writing a book on quitting.)

He reasoned that the increased cost of living in Hawaii would eat up his raise in pay. He questioned if he was ready for such a higher level of responsibility... despite the fact that he had been craving increased responsibility for the last three years. He talked about the fact that he might get sick from the heat. Finally, I confronted Ken and told him that he was simply fearing the change.

Ken never did go to Hawaii. But his life had one significant change. A year later he found that he had a bleeding ulcer. This changed his diet, his attitude, and his life — significantly. I am thankful that Ken has given me permission to use his story, because he believes that he might have avoided this ulcer if he had followed his heart instead of his fear.

In relationships and marriage, the fear of change keeps together people who should have parted long ago. While there are few things more beautiful than a loving, nourishing and fulfilling relationship, there few things more devastating than a relationship lacking these qualities.

Some people do get out of relationships too quickly, of course. Many fail to explore their relationships fully and regret their quick exit.

One of the saddest examples of the staying syndrome is those people who remain together in a lousy relationship because they fear being alone. They have been conditioned to believe that no matter how bad their relationship might be, being out of a relationship has got to be worse.

It rarely is.

Those who have risked major life changes realize — *once they have made the change* — that there was almost nothing to fear. Fear of change is an irrational fear — like the fear of falling off the end of the world. Yet, for "more of the same" many will give up the opportunity for a higher income. For this predictability, dead relationships remain dead. Some will even sacrifice much of their well being for a guarantee that things will remain the same.

STAYING REASON NUMBER EIGHT:
"What Would Everyone Say?"

Many people find it hard to admit they are experiencing this fear. Even though we may actually fear the opinions of others, most of us have a hard time admitting it.

Growing up, you might have been conditioned to seek the approval of others. If you became a well-conditioned subject, you feel much better when someone approves of what you do. Conversely, you feel bad when that approval is withheld. Consider what might have happened if the following people would have needed the approval of others in order to feel their self-worth:

Come on, Mr. Bach. What's this I hear about your wanting to write cantatas and concertos? You're an organist — one of the best organists in Germany. What will people think if you start talking about giving that up?

Thomas, you gotta face reality. How many times have you tried that stupid idea for an electric light? It must be more than a thousand times now. People are starting to talk.

Aw, Copernicus, how many experts do we have to parade in front of you to get you off that silly idea. The sun goes around the earth. How can a man with your intelligence think the earth goes around the sun?

L.S. Barksdale, creator of the Barksdale Self-Esteem Programs, claims that you will not have total self-esteem until you are free of being concerned with what others think of you. This does not mean that you don't respect their opinions. It does not mean that you refuse to listen to what they have to say. But, it does mean that when decision time comes, the only expert on you is you.

STAYING REASON NUMBER NINE:
"I'm Needed Here"

Loyalty is one of the qualities of the good Boy Scout. Our society teaches and rewards loyalty under almost all circumstances. "My country right or wrong" grows in popularity whenever a wave of patriotism rises. Schools expect loyalty from students even if those same schools are not willing to give loyalty in return. The same is true of a majority of jobs. People in relationships and marriage expect loyalty from their partners.

Loyalty is a wonderful trait, one which most of us admire in ourselves and in others. Because it is such a positive trait, it can easily be used to manipulate people into staying in bad environments.

In these circumstances it is not the loyalty which hurts. It is actually a misunderstood concept of loyalty, a one-sided loyalty. An unfaithful husband may expect his wife to remain loyal to the marriage even though he lacks the same commitment or fidelity. A boss may expect total loyalty; whereas he has no intention of being loyal to the people under him. A company may expect loyalty from its workers, yet anytime feel it can transfer them or lay them off.

A minister friend of mine was told for eighteen years that as a Methodist minister his loyalty was expected, and Orin was loyal. Yet when he was unjustly accused of child molestation, his bishop "dumped" Orin like a hot potato. He was suspended without pay and removed from his church.

When he was declared innocent after his trial, the bishop told him he could apply for another church. Orin had the following to say to the bishop: "Where was your loyalty? Where were you — my leaders — when I needed you most?"

Orin left the Methodist ministry and pursued a career in teaching.

Such one-way loyalty is expected — but not earned. Nothing other than the privilege of remaining is given in return. A worker who gets an ulcer working too hard for his company gets to come back for more of the same — as long as he remains loyal. A woman who has been abused in a relationship gets to come back for more; however, if she is not loyal, she might lose that "privilege."

If this sounds absurd, please be aware that many reading this book are now experiencing pangs of recognition. They realize that all they have received for their loyalty is *more of what they do not want*. Such loyalty does not come from within; it is an effect of manipulation, achieving what someone else wants. If you are "loyal," you will leave the town that you love and go where the company sends you. If you are "loyal," you will stay in the marriage or relationship which is draining you of all of your strength. If you are "loyal," you will continue to take all of the abuse because that is what other "loyal" people are doing.

In your own social analysis, ask yourself if your loyalty is appreciated or expected. If it is just expected, there is a good chance that that is a false loyalty which is being used more for manipulation than motivation.

Ask yourself if the loyalty which is expected of you is returned by the person or organization expecting the loyalty. If the loyalty is not returned to the degree it is expected, your situation is out of balance.

Ask yourself whether the loyalty expected from you comes from an established tradition or is something which comes from realistic expectations. If this expectation comes in a good environment, that probably means that loyalty works both ways.

(It must have taken a lot of loyalty for the workers of Delta Airlines, on their own initiative, to buy an airplane for their company. I have talked to many Delta employees, each of whom has assured me that the idea was his or her own and a very easy thing to do. According to all whom I interviewed, Delta is a very happy place to work. Thus, their loyalty was a positive response to a positive environment.)

Ask yourself if the loyalty you give now was at one time good and natural. At one time you may have responded to considerate management or a sensitive partner. However, circumstances do change. The conditions which inspired the loyalty may no longer exist. Sometimes a situation will erode so slowly that a person does not consciously realize what is happening. This is why probing a situation and one's feelings about it are so important.

STAYING REASON NUMBER TEN:
"I Don't Want to Be Selfish"

The word "selfish" makes much more of an emotional impact than most realize; thus, it is a superb manipulation tool. Yet, "selfish" garners its impact more from ignorance than from understanding.

What exactly does selfish mean? If we accept the stock definition of "pertaining to the self," that means that we are all selfish people. However, the commonly accepted meaning suggests egotism: concerned with our needs to such a degree that other's needs are excluded. The father who deserts his wife and children after cleaning out his bank account is selfish. Few disagree with that view.

However, what about the father who's had it with a job which no longer rewards him? Is he selfish because he wants something better? Those prone to quick judgement couldn't care less about the context of the situation. If this father has provided a secure and comfortable home, his exploration of new possibilities could be interpreted as selfish. However, if he has just had a stroke and a doctor orders him to find other work, none will consider him selfish. An "acceptable" personal tragedy has validated his move.

Note the words: "acceptable personal tragedy." We still live in a society where many do not consider misery in one's work or in a relationship, or lack of fulfillment in one's career, to constitute an "acceptable personal tragedy." The fact that few people use their talents to the fullest is not considered a personal tragedy.

This waste of talent makes living in such a society a potential tragedy — a tragedy compounded by placing the "selfish" label on those who dare to remove themselves from such a circumstance.

That's exactly what selfish is... a label. Labels rarely have anything to do with reality. Yet, they can block communication when it is most needed.

Richard was an executive with a Fortune 500 company. His description of his job — non-nourishing and cutthroat — was probably an understatement. People above him made demands of him twelve hours a day, six days a week. People under him complained more than they cooperated. In a conversation he recounted to me how he had been trying for two years to talk to his wife about his desire to move into a more fulfilling job:

R: "Every time I bring the subject up, Mary puts her hands over her ears and refuses to listen. I don't know how many times she has said that my wanting to get out is selfish."

JB: "What is it that you would really like to do?"

R: "What I really want to do is find a product which I really believe in and sell it. I would eventually make more, but the transition period would be rough. I couldn't ask Mary and the kids to put up with that."

JB: "Put up with what?"

R: "The lower standard of living."

JB: "Are you the only one making money in the family?"

R: "Yes."

JB: "Only you can determine how to make that money."

R: "No, you don't understand. Look what I would be doing to my family."

JB: "Look at what you are doing to yourself."

R: "But it would be selfish to ask them to make that sacrifice."

This conversation reveals the conditioning which manipulates us with labels which we desperately do not want to have pinned on us no matter how false they are. Richard did not think that his wife was selfish for wanting to maintain their high standard of living. (And she wasn't.) However, he thought he was selfish for wanting to find more fulfilling work.

Susan was a nun in a convent for twelve years. She felt selfish because she wanted to leave. She wanted to serve God; yet she wanted to do it in the business world. She could never get over the feeling that she was letting God down, thus being selfish by leaving the convent.

Harry hated the high powered company where he worked. He did not enjoy the people or the pace. Yet his father had founded the company and hoped Harry would take over. Wanting to pursue something else, Harry felt selfish.

Milly is president of the women's group at a large Baptist church, having been a member of the church for more than twenty years. However, the church now has a minister who has driven most of her friends away. Only the "hell and damnation" people are left. Millie finds that she can no longer relate to the gossip which is now a large part of the meetings. Milly desperately wants out of her office and that church; yet she feels leaving would be selfish.

Some one-sided books do overemphasize looking out for yourself. Yet, few books emphasize the reality that the more you look after yourself, the more you will be able to meet the needs of others. As an unhappy man, Richard is not providing the image of the complete and loving father. Susan is not really serving God with full effectiveness if she is miserable remaining in the convent. Harry is not going to benefit from working in his father's company if he does not enjoy the environment there. Milly is not doing anyone a favor by remaining the president of a group where she no longer enjoys the people.

STAYING REASON NUMBER ELEVEN:
"My Needs Aren't Important"
Many people feel that their sense of worth increases when they sacrifice for someone else. While this doesn't represent a majority of people, there are enough in the minority to insure the tenure of this mentality.

I realize that I may offend a number of people by daring to suggest that sacrifice rarely works. In fact, I suggest that when you make a sacrifice for someone, there exists a high possibility that everyone will lose. How can someone win when you have to give up something? I accept that many people do this and have allowed themselves to feel good about it. However, that in no way assures that the sacrifice is actually beneficial.

Numerous studies reveal that students who have little or no financial help from their parents do much better in college. Those who have their full way paid benefit the least. Still, parents think it is their duty to pay for their children's higher education. There are many good reasons for helping to pay for a child's education, and I am not going to get into those. What I want to point out is a very bad — and even common — situation: remaining in a personally destructive job or situation so that the funds will be available for a child's education.

I remember a mother and daughter who were in one of my college classes. The mother felt the father was noble for postponing his decision to move to another job until Carolyn completed college. One time during a conference with the daughter, I asked:

JB: "How would you feel if your father left his job and looked for something better?"

C: "I would be so relieved. Dad doesn't realize how unhappy he is. But Mom and I know. So many times I have wanted to tell him that I would do just fine, but I just don't know how to bring the subject up."

JB: "So you wouldn't feel that he was copping out on an obligation?"

C: "I'd much rather see him happy like he used to be when he was younger."

Carolyn felt guilty about her father's sacrifice. She had not been consulted. *From her viewpoint no one was winning*. I finally urged the mother to get the message to her husband that things were not going to fall apart if he gave up his "noble" sacrifice.

The nobility of sacrifice tends to be overrated because intelligent alternatives are not considered. Conditioned to think that sacrifice is noble, we often fail to think through the consequences when we consider making sacrifices for others. How will the other person feel? How about the potential guilt which that person might experience? Might the "sacrifice" deny the other person a sense of accomplishment? Is the sacrifice treating everyone fairly? Is it honest?

A person staying in a deteriorating relationship or marriage because there is great concern for the other person may appear noble — however, the potential for an even greater disaster lies ahead.

A mother stays in a marriage "for the sake of the children," yet some studies have shown such a situation to be ineffective and sometimes even harmful to all concerned. Parents who make such sacrifices for their children — even younger children — put pressure on those children at a time in their lives when they don't need it. Many social workers feel that the children would be far better off mentally if each parent were happier as a result of a necessary separation.

In relationships and marriage, sacrifice often becomes a war cry. The idea that sacrifice is essential to make a relationship work is based more on conditioning than logic, and may well be counterproductive. When *commitment* is substituted for sacrifice, relationships are based on a more nourishing foundation.

Chapter 9.

"Winners Never Quit" — and Other Myths

Humans love myths. Since the beginning of recorded history, myths have been used to explain anything which was not understood. Cultures have developed elaborate mythologies to socialize their members. Religions have employed myths to reinforce their belief systems. Societies find myths useful to engender patriotism, loyalty, hard work, ...and staying.

As you continue to explore your own situation, it will help to recognize the myths which influence staying. Friends and family members will give advice derived from these myths. Most will be well-meant. The problem is, this advice will be based on myth, not reality.

Whether concerned with quitting or staying, people will tell you the truth as they see it. Even if these myths have validity for them, that does not mean that they will have validity for you. The buck does not stop with the one advising.

What follows are some of the more invalid and destructive myths you will encounter. Forewarned is forearmed. They are meant to be part of your analysis.

One final word about myths. Most have their foundation in truth. For your unique circumstances, they might have validity. In no way am I suggesting that myth equals lie. Be bold enough to accept that someone else's truth could be a lie for you. For you, myth has validity only if it confirms your own experience.

MYTH NUMBER ONE:

"Winners Never Quit   —   Quitters Never Win"

This has to be one of the most stirring quotes in the English language. It is also one of the most stupid. It can be highly manipulative and is usually stated by someone who has run out of rational ways to motivate a person.

Winners do quit at times. Quitting actually helped them to become greater winners.

In biographies of famous people you will see that many recognized a dead end and had the courage to move on. Some realized that they had crawled out too far on a non-productive limb and needed to retreat. Some accepted that they had learned all they could from an experience and recognized the need to move in another direction. They did not become winners because they refused to quit. They became winners because they *knew when to quit*.

There is another part to the myth — quitters never win. Since this is a cliche among sports professionals, a couple of sports examples might provide some clarity. Baseball managers have privately said that they might win ten more games a year if pitchers were willing to confess when they know they don't have it anymore. But that would be quitting, for heaven's sake! Thus, the manager is forced into the role of mind reader.

Many retired football players admit that they stuck it out a year or two too long. Some remained long enough to do themselves great physical harm. However, the money was good, and who can resist the cheers of the crowd. Summing it up beautifully, one player said: "I wish I had quit when I was a winner."

In relationships and marriage, quitting can indicate that there is no more hope. Who knows that better than the two involved? If the partners try a trial separation before too much harm has been done, a marriage might be saved. This process of "partial" quitting provides time for clarity and introspection.

On the job, workers have the right to use their training and talent. If they are unfulfilled and unable to use their skills, the expression "Quitters never win" is a lie. Each person has the obligation to self and to loved ones — to move to a more fulfilling opportunity. Here, quitting is a cure and not something to be scorned.

MYTH NUMBER TWO:
"You Will Regret This for the Rest of Your Life"

I would not have even bothered to include this ridiculous statement except for its massive repetition. Such a statement reflects an "imminent disaster" mentality, suggesting that even if the quit is premature, or turns out to be a mistake, that the situation cannot be turned to the person's advantage.

Such a statement used to be standard advice to people seeking divorce. Our society is a little more enlightened now. Folks used to say this to people who had made the decision not to go to college. Now, statistics reveal that those without college degrees are doing almost as well — financially at least — as those with degrees.

Well-meaning friends will say, "You're making a big mistake!" when one considers leaving an environment where he or she has been comfortable. It may be changing political parties. It may be your decision to move from being a Baptist to being a Mormon. (Here some believers might be tempted to say this is a mistake which will be regretted for all of eternity.) It may be the decision to leave a small prestigious college and go to a large state university.

Others have made costly decisions. Galileo was told to cease his explorations into the idea that the Earth went around the sun. He was taken on a tour of the inquisition chambers and shown the most gruesome devices of torture. He was old and feared the excruciating pain. Thus, he decided to recant his theories. He appraised the cost and found it to be too high. It was a decision which came from within and with the knowledge that once the furor was over he could publish his theories under another name in another country.

The people I've interviewed after they have made quitting decisions have only one consistent area of regret: that they did not quit sooner.

MYTH NUMBER THREE:
"Quitting Is a Selfish Act"

There *are* times when quitting is selfish. To quit is selfish when the person thinks *only* of himself, and isn't willing to consider that others might be hurt.

A selfish quitter might tell her family, "I've had enough of this area; I've decided that we're going to live in Arizona." The rest of the family is not consulted. There is no concern whether they would be happy living in a desert area. There is no concern about the children leaving school in the middle of the year, or whether all members of the family would be healthy in the new environment. The announcement is made, and the family is expected to follow. This is a fairly good example of quitting as a selfish act. However, *it is not the quitting which is selfish.* It is instead the blunt and callous way this person treats her family.

Self-validation is not the same as selfishness. In a self-validating move, there is always concern for the other people involved.

"Selfish," for many, is a blanket term covering any situation where a person considers his or her personal needs. For those who cannot separate selfishness from self-validation, it does not matter whether the person has made an effort to consider others. The person who is acting according to personal needs will be judged selfish.

Most people on the brink of quitting will consider themselves selfish as a result of social conditioning — the messages with which society bombards us. There are some realities which can help us debunk this myth:

- It is almost impossible to make a totally unselfish quitting decision. Someone is always going to be affected.

- In a relationship or marriage, it is almost impossible to have both agree that quitting the relationship would be a good idea.

- Selfish is *always* a label. It is very difficult to find agreement on what is selfish and what is not.

- Failing to do something because of the fear of being labelled selfish is self-defeating.

MYTH NUMBER FOUR:
"Time Heals All Wounds"

This myth does indeed have a nice ring to it. However, it too is often a lie, used as manipulation to stop movement and thought.

If time heals wounds, it also deepens them.

Lynn began her career as a high school teacher in San Diego. She had an especially rough first six weeks. While no one offered to help her with her excessive work load, many offered a continuous barrage of advice. The core of the advice was, "Hang in there, because it is always rough for a first year teacher." While the statement is true, in relationship to Lynn's situation, it was a lie because it implied that Lynn's problems would diminish as she gained experience.

Lynn simply was not cut out to be a teacher. She didn't really like the kids. She was bored with the other teachers and their security-obsessed mentality. She didn't have the slightest interest in the political aspects of her profession. She did like her subject, but not enough to dilute it for her students.

What Lynn did enjoy was three months off in the summer. During that period she reassured herself that the worst was over — exactly what every teacher said. Believing this, she began her second year. Within six weeks she was deeply depressed. When a good number of her colleagues told her that "things really don't get good until the beginning of the third year," something within Lynn snapped. Nine weeks into her second year, Lynn resigned.

For Lynn, time did not heal anything.

Time actually increased her nightmare.

A nightmare can also be continued in a relationship. Both may know inside that the relationship can't be healed. Yet, they may cling to the hope that time will be their healer. If the people themselves can't heal their relationships, time sure cannot.

There is, however, one area where time will heal the wounds. When a person who has left a bad relationship or marriage feels a devastating sense of loss, time is almost always a healer. The sense of loss will diminish, and self-esteem increase with time.

MYTH NUMBER FIVE:
"Security Is More Important Than Fulfillment"

You'll not likely hear this myth at all... until you reveal your intention to quit.

We live in a security-obsessed society. Most jobs provide medical insurance, dental insurance, extended illness insurance, etc. People on strike demand a guarantee that they will always have a job. It doesn't matter that fewer people buy their product. It may not even matter if productivity has drastically dwindled.

A few years ago I talked to the personnel manager of a large company. He had worked with his company for fifteen years:

> *When I began working here, the people I interviewed wanted to be sure that they would be using their skills and education. They wanted to know what the chances for upward movement were. They wanted to know if their ideas would be heard. Now they want to be assured that they will be taken care of when they retire thirty-five years down the line. They want to know if the medical plan will cover the cost of drugs and if the dental plan will cover the cost of gold. They want to be sure that if they are sick, they will get their full salary. This is a very security-conscious group.*

If you have bought into the "security over fulfillment" mentality, it may be hard to quit the most abusive situations. The threat of lost security may cause you to remain with someone who mentally, or even physically, abuses you.

The more you *need* security, the more vulnerable you make yourself. With such a mentality the idea of quitting will always be a threat. You will be tempted to tolerate more than is good for you. You will stay longer until it hurts more. Instead of pursuing personal freedom, quitting will be associated with personal disaster. A security obsession could actually lead to your own personal depression.

Countless clients have told their marriage counselors that they remained with partners who mentally and physically abused them, despite the fact that they were not safe. So great was their need to feel secure, they remained in non-nourishing and sometimes devastating relationships. Other men and women have felt intense pangs of boredom, yet have remained with their spouses because the loss of security appeared too terrifying. This mentality clouds the vision of something better, and the willingness to explore for it.

Loss of security can make a good excuse to avoid quitting. Avoid making security a priority until other issues have been explored, so your quitting decision can be approached with more clarity.

****

Old ideas die hard. For too long a time, people thought the Earth was flat. Now we readily recognize that a curved shadow on the moon should have told our ancestors better. (Of course that's easier to understand for a generation which has seen the Earth from space!)

So it is with myths which influence our social structure. In his PBS-TV series, "The Day the Universe Changed," James Burke dramatized a harrowing witch trial, claiming that what we now realize was *myth* was at that time *reality* to both accuser and accused. Despite the very strong belief, these myths served no one.

In prison camps during the Korean conflict, three times as many American prisoners (per capita) died of the cold because they subscribed to a myth that sleeping three or four to a sleeping bag to conserve warmth was "weird." The

South Korean prisoners had a better chance of survival because they did not "buy into" such a myth.

Your chances for making the best decision — whether it be quitting or staying — will depend a lot on how much you focus on what will best serve you and your loved ones, and how much you can avoid buying into myths which don't hold up.

Decision

Chapter 10.

Discovering the Message of Crisis

Most moves which lead to success are preceded by a crisis. Being fired from a job can be a prelude to disaster or a wonderfully significant opportunity. A broken relationship or divorce can be such a crushing blow that the person can appear helpless for weeks... even months. Or that same event can be the impetus for a leap to a much more fulfilling experience.

Crisis stands as a potential friend, and almost always carries a message within it. While the message speaks in many tongues, it always has the same theme:

You have lost touch — it's time to move to something better.

Ignored messages often get stronger, and cause a crisis to intensify. A force within doesn't want to let go. A compassionate voice urges you to move on, to embrace what is uniquely you.

Sadly, many folks try to quiet this voice. Yielding to conditioning that says, "numb that pain," they resort to drugs, therapy, or even good old fashioned "coping." But numbing such an important message actually increases the potential for depression and tension.

One level of crisis is a direct response to something which has already happened (the loss of a loved one or a financial disaster.) This crisis is usually brought on by an event such as death in the family or being fired from a job. This level of crisis centers around a decision which has already been made or an event which has already happened.

The level of crisis which centers around a quitting or staying decision has you in the driver's seat. You could be in a job where you have gone as far as you can go; little potential for challenge or fulfillment exists. You might need — perhaps even thrive on — stronger and more personal challenges. The continuation of what you are doing only promises greater boredom, and your crisis centers around an inner message to move to something better.

In a relationship or marriage this level of crisis does not come from a loss of funds or a severe illness. It comes instead from a deep feeling inside that something within the relationship needs to be better... much better.

Impression Without Expression... Crisis?

Despite having a wonderful job and the esteem of your friends, something inside of you might be telling you that this is a good time to move on to something better. Despite a relationship or marriage which looks good on the surface, something portends that all is not right. Even though you can't explain it rationally, the feeling won't go away.

You've felt this inner gnawing many times in your life.

You may have completed an application to a certain college and then not felt completely right about it. Everything in the catalog was fine. A lot of your friends were considering this prestigious and and highly ranked school. Yet, something within you said that it was not the place for you.

Another time you listened to someone giving you advice about a certain problem. You trusted this person. Because she had guided you well before, you were sure the advice was valid. Yet, this time something stirred deep within. You trusted the person, but not the advice.

You may have been successful in a certain situation for a number of years: a group of friends whom you've known for a long time; a church or religion you have grown up with; a project into which you've put a lot of time and effort. Yet now that feeling is there — "Something is no longer working" — and that feeling won't go away.

When this inner feeling speaks, you could...

...talk to a priest, pastor or rabbi and be assured that everything is okay.

...enter therapy and treat your inner voice as a disturbance instead of a message.

...take a tranquilizer and at least feel better about your circumstances.

...shut it out.

...decide not to trust it.

Each of the above options urges you to ignore what is coming from within, reinforcing belief that outer voices are more important than your own inner voices.

You have other options, of course. You can...

...use a counselor, minister or friend as a sounding board to sense what you are really feeling.

...ask yourself: "Am I *really* doing what I want to do?"

...ask yourself what you really want from life and try to determine how close you are to it.

...consider moving toward a job or relationship which accurately reflects your growth and experience.

You have to work hard at discovering, interpreting and responding to the messages which come from within yourself. Betty was quite comfortable in her well-paying secretarial job, with medical and dental insurance, paid sick leave, and an ideal working environment. Any ideas about quitting would have to be interpreted as neurosis. Yet, the urge to quit was exactly the inner message Betty began to receive.

Betty immediately sought therapy, searching for a neurotic foundation for her crisis. Was it her marriage? Her children? Her childhood? (How had she really felt about her mother?)

When a well meaning friend warned Betty that therapists were "tragically limited to this lifetime," and that she should try past life regression therapy, Betty began to accept that maybe there was nothing wrong with *her* after all!

Betty started paying closer attention to her feelings of dissatisfaction. She noted it most when she was unable to make suggestions at work. She often came home full of ideas about how her office could improve its productivity, but couldn't bring herself to tell her bosses. Such an action she had considered "improper" for a secretary; yet now she realized her inhibition was the foundation of her crisis. She had been "hiding her light under a bushel."

She made an appointment with her boss and told him:

> *I feel I have a lot more talents than I am using on this job. Each day I watch you guys doing things which you don't appear to actively think about. Yet they are costing this company a lot of money. If you could swallow your pride, I think I could help you with this.*

The boss gave her a perfunctory "thanks for sharing," and nothing changed. Her frustration increasing, Betty began looking for work elsewhere. After a few weeks word of her search leaked to her boss. When he confronted her, Betty fired full shot:

*Six weeks ago I talked to you about ways to increase
the productivity of this office. You were polite and
condescending. The strong message was "How a could
lowly secretary contribute anything in this area?" I'm
tired of having talents which I can't use. I'm tired of
not being able to grow. I would like to give you one
very clear message — use me or lose me!*

They decided to use her. She was promoted and given
more responsibility. She had listened to the messages within
herself, and was ready to make a move if that became
necessary.

Betty's story has its own message: if you hear inner
messages, at least explore them. Don't wait for a deeper crisis
to motivate movement.

Crisis in Relationships and Marriage

Relationship crises can speak to you a little differently
because of the high expectations many have about
male-female relationships.

In the media, conflicts are solved very quickly —
twenty-five minutes in most T.V. sitcoms! Avoiding the
deeper aspects of marriage, the media provide an overly
simplistic view of relationships. Unrealistic media-induced
expectations about relationships and marriage help create
crisis in our society. Yet, some partners don't clearly
differentiate between the media image and their personal
reality. When a genuine crisis occurs, it must be heeded if the
relationship and those involved are to grow to much higher
levels — without needing to quit.

For those involved in a shaky marriage or relationship,
the inner feelings might be expressed like this:

I don't know if there's any hope in this relationship.

Our relationship is a lot worse that I thought.

I've been stifling myself for a long time, and it doesn't feel good.

Or the messages might come in a more positive form:

If we work at it, this relationship can be much better.

Our marriage has the potential for a far greater love.

I can experience a more unique me in this relationship.

Deeper thought and honest inner reflection can lead to communication which helps save a marriage or relationship. *This is also a form of quitting.* You are quitting old patterns which no longer work for you.

Crisis and Work

Gradually, our society seems to be recognizing that the idea of "only one career for a lifetime" is no longer valid. With increased technology, new careers emerge. With greater personal freedom of choice and more career options, many individuals are seeking more fulfillment from their jobs. A new career might use your talents far more effectively that the one you're in now.

A crisis can point the way to better conditions. Something within could be pushing you to search for ways to experience even greater fulfillment. Sometimes, it is a volcano within. If blocked, its energy can be destructive. Yet, channeled with increased awareness, that same energy could move you to a much more meaningful life.

If you are a salesperson, perhaps you will find yourself increasingly bored with your own presentation. You find the people you are selling to uninteresting. The sales meetings are now deadly dull.

If you are a company executive, the challenge of making the job and the company work may be fading, Planning strategy becomes more chore than challenge. Long periods of overtime become increasingly annoying.

If you are a homemaker, you find the house starting to close in. You love your kids, but — by God — they've been getting to you lately. No matter how sensitive your spouse, you're not getting out enough. Driving your kids to school was something you once did automatically. No more. Now each chore is a *chore*.

The Message of Crisis

Crises provide opportunities for transformation, helping us realize that what worked before is no longer working.

The message of a crisis may be, "There is a much better way for you, and you are not moving in that direction." If you begin to hear the inner message of crisis in your life, you could...

...shut off the message with drugs.

...seek therapy and "cure" the message.

...analyse the message to death and learn absolutely nothing from it.

...talk about it to the point where the conversation becomes more important than the growth.

Or you could put conditions on your potential for growth:

I'll grow as long as it doesn't interfere with my security.

I'll grow as long as it is comfortable.

I'll grow as long as I don't have to give up any past beliefs.

I'll grow as long as I don't have to change.

There is a better alternative: a life crisis as an important message from yourself urging you to move to something better. This time pay attention. Let your own feelings lead you to move in a more self-validating direction, or to explore what it is you really want.

Trust what you are feeling. Chances are very good that your desire for something better is very healthy. The chances are slim that you are immature for wanting to quit — or wanting to improve your situation. A "deeper voice" in you just might know better. It's worth it to listen to that voice (unless it's suggesting that you do harm to yourself or others. If that is the sort of message you're hearing, I urge you to find a professional therapist to talk it over with).

Chapter 11.

Some Thoughts About Seeking Advice

Let's face it: good advice is very difficult to come by.

Much advice will be offered; little will meet your needs. You have a distinct frame of reference and a singular experience. Even those who know you best lack your unique perspective. Any advice will always come from *their* frame of reference. Indeed, people who know you well — even those who genuinely care about you — could give you some incredibly bad advice.

What is tempting you to seek advice? Your situation no longer feels right. You are considering a move which may appear drastic. It feels to you as though it would help to talk it over with others. Would it? Perhaps, sometimes, for some people. Caveat: *advisee beware!*

Good advisors will urge you to talk about your problem. They understand your need to have a sounding board. Realizing that your background and experience are unique, they try to understand that background before offering any advice. They avoid giving blanket advice. They do their best to avoid giving their personal beliefs and instead urge you to work within yours. They understand that only *you* have to live with your decision. Because of this, they advise with wisdom and compassion.

The purpose for seeking advice is *not* to be told what to do. If you need someone to tell you what to do, you probably are not ready to make a decision. You should seek advice mainly to gain more insight. *Good* advice will lead you to new insights.

If within five minutes of a discussion you hear, "You know what I would do if I were you?" it's time to seek another advisor.

Why Seeking Advice May Not Be Productive

For the next few pages, let's explore why seeking advice may be counter-productive. Consider some reasons why it *might* (at least in the beginning stages) be better to go it alone. (This does not mean that I am advising you to go it alone. That would make *me* an advisor who is insensitive to your experience and frame of reference!) However, at least consider some reasons why avoiding advice is sometimes a good idea.

Each of the title-statements which follow represents a potential pitfall which can come from seeking the advice of others. Some of these statements might appear absurd. Others may appear absurd until your own experience confirms them. My guess is that you've heard most of them before:

"I Don't Think You Should Quit Right Now."

Because of the widespread belief that quitting is bad, it is not easy to find an advisor who is free of this opinion. Remember that *you* have been in deep thought about your situation; this is the first time your advisor is aware of your feelings.

At the point I was in one of the worst jobs of my teaching career, I wrote a very close friend asking for advice. Here is his final paragraph:

Jack, you are a selfish person. You have a very strong personality which gets you in trouble. You are going to have to learn to back off if you are going to survive. There is no way that you are going to find a better job. Stay in there and take the lumps.

In another environment this might have been good advice. Many times compromises have contributed to my knowledge and growth; both school and teacher have won. However, in this situation no compromise or growth was possible. I was not allowed to use modern teaching techniques which I had spent years developing and had been promised I could use. I was falsely accused of trying to turn the younger teachers against the administration, and despite total lack of proof for this accusation, most administrators continued to believe it. They watched me like hawks. Other teachers sensed higher enthusiasm and competence in my students' writing, but I was still considered ineffective as a teacher and dangerous as a person.

Thus, in this context, with no chance for growth on either side, my friend's counsel to "stay in there and take the lumps" was *bad* advice. Yet, I deferred my thoughts about quitting because I had faith in this friend (and still do). He had given me good advice before, and I considered his ideas valid.

If you are thinking about quitting a job, remember: most people around you at work are planning to stay. Chances are you'll get lots of "hang in there" advice. Staying may be perfect for them. *You* are the one with the inner rumblings.

If a colleague is not happy with his job and is staying, he

might be threatened by the fact that you are planning to break free.

If a co-worker just feels '"okay" about her job, she may want you to stick around so she can have company. (As cynical as this may sound, it is a very human response.)

A work-mate who feels good about his job may have difficulty understanding your problem.

In relationships and marriage, you will experience the same problem. If your advisor had six different relationships in the last year, she won't understand why your relationship is deteriorating for the first time in five years.

If you seek the advice of someone who has been unhappy yet remained within a bad marriage, you can expect advice to stay.

The problem is that the advice of these well-meaning friends might come from an obsession with *staying* rather than a concern for *healing*. Advisors who have that focus on healing are worth their weight in gold.

"What's Best For You May Be Selfish"

Almost anybody you ask will try to give the best advice possible. Nevertheless, "doing-what-you-really-want-is-selfish" conditioning is really powerful.

Some advisors might say it this way: "Sometimes you've got to sacrifice doing what you really love to do." Another might say: "You're thinking of yourself too much; why don't you think of others?"

The advice may be sincere... perhaps even effective. However, there are droves of advisors who believe that personal need — just about any personal need — is selfish, and that such a need should be subordinated to the job or relationship.

While this mentality might have worked for Genghis Khan, it has potentially disastrous consequences today:

A minister could be advised to conquer his situation when a new career might be best.

A harrassed and non-nourished married woman could be advised to stay in the relationship because the advisor personally believes that duty comes before happiness.

A businessman could be advised to remain in a bad job because the advisor denied his own needs in order to be a good "company man."

People do not intentionally advise you to go against your greatest good. However, they might consider your "greatest good" to come from denying your strongest personal needs. They hide such biases under the label of "doing what is best." They may not understand your inner turmoil. They just might be advising you to do what they believe is "right," rather than what is *best*.

"Things Are Bound To Get Better If You Stay."

If you know there is no hope, there is no need to seek advice. If you are confused about the potential for hope, the advice you receive may overinflate hope's possibility. You may be at the point of acknowledging defeat — not because you are a quitter, but because you have surveyed your situation and found it hopeless.

Courage has led you to consider quitting. Yet, as you expose yourself to a person lacking empathy, you might find your resolve waning. When you considered your own experience, you knew what you had to do. Now someone not even close to your experience recommends that you stay — at least for a little while longer. The problem is "a little while longer" sometimes becomes a broken record, stretching out for a seeming eternity. Essential momentum for your decision could be lost.

In relationships and marriage, advice to remain hopeful abounds, no matter what the situation. Romance is always an influential factor, of course, and the romantic view pervades. What's more, few people have actual "'ogres'" as partners, so the potential for some change is usually possible. (There *are* a few ogres, of course; if your partner is one, your decision is easier!) You need to get beyond the romance and inertia and think clearly, so you can determine if your relationship is worth saving.

Much advice avoids the here-and-now of the relationship, focusing instead on the past or future:

Remember how nicely she used to treat you.

He's going to get better once things improve at the office.

There was a time when you guys were so lovey-dovey. You can recapture that.

Here are some answers to the previous statements which are justifiable in many circumstances — maybe yours:

He isn't treating me nicely now, and he hasn't for a long time.

Things have improved at the office, but they haven't improved here.

We've tried to recapture that lovey-dovey feeling. It hasn't worked.

The above answers reflect an acknowledgement of hopelessness. They may not represent answers to your own situation; however, if any of them touched off feelings within you, take some time now to explore those feelings. Write about them in your log or journal. Take another look at the questions in Chapters 4 - 7. Use this awareness as an opportunity to move toward greater clarity about your situation.

"Just Be Patient; Persevere."

Patience and perseverance could be elements of good advice you receive. However, they could simply reflect the advisor's frame of reference.

Ruth thought seriously about getting out of her engagement. Dan was basically a "salt of the earth" person, and Ruth realized that she had been swept off her feet by his charm and masculinity. Within six weeks they were engaged. Two weeks into the engagement, however, Ruth realized that Dan did not possess the cultural background he claimed. She became greatly concerned when he slept through most of a Los Angeles Philharmonic concert.

Whatever Ruth's concern, the advice given her usually translated into "patience and perseverance." A friend of Dan's said that patience would help her accept Dan's lack of culture, his belching, and his foul mouth. If Ruth could just persevere, she would eventually see his good. Another friend said that Dan was "a fox" and that she should "hang in there," because few men were as good looking. Ruth's mother also urged patience.

Amidst this flurry of advice, Ruth found herself enjoying Dan less and less. Dan managed to be highly charming when he was around other people. When he was alone with Ruth, the charm faded. Yet only one of her advisors found this relevant.

Ruth took the advice and remained with Dan despite an increasing dread of being with him. When Ruth tried to talk about what was bothering her, Dan laughed it off, saying, "Nobody's perfect." Neither was the advice. Six weeks before the marriage, Ruth went crying to her mother:

Mom, I just don't love him any more. I don't even like him. I don't enjoy being with him.

The advice she received? More variations on the theme of perseverance and patience:

Ruth, I didn't feel that your father had to be perfect when I married him. He had faults, but I persevered. If I had let those faults stop me, I could have ruined our marriage. If I had not been patient, I might have missed out on someone you and I both know is a wonderful man. I know there is some real good in Dan. If you will have patience, you'll eventually be able to see it.

Ruth felt doomed. She waited three more weeks. Seeing no change in the pattern, she ended the relationship.

In the workplace, patience and perseverance are also almost universally advised. Too often that advice shows little respect for individual needs.

Steve was told that in his job he had gone as far as a non-degreed person could go. (He was a foreman for a Philadelphia oil company.) He knew that he had the talent and skills to move to a higher level of responsibility. For many, this would have been inspiration enough to look elsewhere. However, Steve felt it was best to seek advice first.

His wife urged him to avoid being hasty and suggested that the company might change its mind. His father agreed that it was a tragedy, but felt that it would be a greater tragedy if Steve moved. Dad's advice: persevere and see what happens — they weren't going to let a good man rust. Steve's boss told him that he was only fifteen years from retirement and that he had a very good position. If he had patience, the company might eventually lift the ban. In a few years he might have a chance for promotion.

Steve considered all of the advice to be "incredibly bad." He began looking around for other work. When he saw how good the possibilities were, he prepared a totally different resume and began asking for letters of recommendation. His superiors were shocked. They felt they had treated Steve well. How could he want to move?

Steve told them to lift the limit immediately.

They didn't.

Steve quit and quickly found another job with good upside potential — more quickly than even he expected. His well-meaning advisors were astonished.

Steve explored by seeking advice. The advice he got did not really help him. What did eventually help him was having the courage to explore the possibilities for a better life for himself and his family. Ironically, no one had advised him to do that. Fortunately, he listened to himself rather than following the counsel of others.

For you, advice is only as good as its contribution to your own personal fulfillment — to being the person you uniquely are. Advice which centers around convention and the *advisor's* personal belief system (instead of *your* unique circumstances) has a very good chance of pulling you off center and creating further confusion.

Choose selectively, listen carefully, evaluate critically, ... and follow your own feelings.

Do You Need to Quit Quitting?

Some folks make a habit of quitting. *Their* rut is an endless series of quits and new beginnings.

You know by now that I certainly do not advocate "hanging in there." However, I do encourage you not to go from one extreme — staying at all costs — to another — quitting every time your "enthusiasm index" drops one point! If quitting is a *pattern* for you, maybe you're not giving yourself *or* your situations enough chance to succeed.

Take a look at the numbers in the next chapter, and see how reasonable your quit/stay decisions really are.

Chapter 12.

The "Knowing When to Quit Index"
An "Objective" Aid for Making Your Decision

Have you decided that you're going to quit? Or have you found that staying works for you? Are you close — ever so close — to a decision? Have you stirred up so many feelings that your mind is too cluttered to decide?

If the jury is still out, this chapter could help you get past the mental clutter. The "Knowing When to Quit Index" will help you determine your best direction.

In Chapters 4 through 7 you answered job or relationship questions centering around four themes:

- Can you stay and still be happy?
- Will you hurt yourself by quitting?
- Will you hurt others by quitting?
- Are you in a nourishing — or toxic — environment?

If you answered the questions posed in those chapters, you had totals for the job-related and/or relationship-related questions. You can now use those collective totals to help you determine whether quitting or staying — or something between the two — would be your best option. The procedures described in this chapter will enable you to use the results of those brief surveys.

Keep in mind that any such "objective" device for decision-making is, at its best, *one tool* to help you reach a conclusion. *Please do not rely solely upon the results of the procedures which follow.* They are intended to help you sort out your own feelings, and should be treated as you might view a thoughtful conversation with yourself — at one point in time. (Indeed, you may wish to answer the questions in Chapters 4 - 7 once again; you'll find them reproduced in the Appendix for that purpose.)

The "Knowing When to Quit Index" is not a standardized psychological test. It has been developed as a result of my work with clients and students who were seeking — as you are — a better way to reach the staying/quitting decision. The scoring procedures are based on my observations of the experiences of people with whom I've worked — not on statistical analysis or other procedures necessary to validate a psychological test. There is no "magic" in these numbers — merely a useful outline to guide you through the difficult and confusing process of deciding whether to stay or quit.

(I'd enjoy hearing from you about how the Index works — or doesn't work — to help bring *you* to a good stay/quit decision. Write me in care of the publisher.)

The balance of this chapter is divided into two "Knowing When to Quit Index" sections: one for jobs and one for relationships. Use either or both, as appropriate to your own situation.

The Knowing When to Quit Index for Jobs and Careers

The following steps provide a procedure for combining your totals for the question sets you completed in Chapters 4 - 7. If you work your way through this process, you'll have a rough total "quit score," which may help you to see more objectively how strong your feelings really are about your job situation.

• Go back to page 37 in Chapter 4 and find your total for the questions you answered "yes." Write that number — Total "J-1" — in the space below.

Total for job related questions from Chapter 4: _____ (J-1)

• Now go back to page 43 in Chapter 5 and find your total of questions answered "yes." Place that number (J-2) in the space below.

Total for job related questions from Chapter 5: _____ (J-2)

• Now go back to page 54 in Chapter 6 and find the total (J-3) of questions you answered "no." Write that number below. (Note: In the previous two groups, you totalled your YES's. In this group — and only this group — you are totalling your NO's.)

Total for job related questions in Chapter 6: _____ (J-3)

• Go to page 62 in Chapter 7 and find the total (J-4) of questions you *left blank*; write that total in the space below. (Note: In each of the other question groups, you totalled the number of items you *checked*. In this group — and only this group — you are totalling the number of items you *left blank*.)

Total nourishing job questions left blank in Chapter 7:
_____ (J-4)

• Also in Chapter 7 you answered questions about how toxic your environment was. Please go to page 63 and find the total (J-5) of times you answered "yes"; write your "J-5" total in the space below:

Total for toxic job questions from Chapter 7: _____ (J-5)

• Now answer the three questions below. These are new questions; you have not done them before.

_____ 1. I really do not feel any better about my job or career since I have been reading this book.

_____ 2. As much as I have looked for light at the end of the tunnel, I really don't see any.

_____ 3. I firmly believe there is much more potential in another job or career.

Total of "yes" answers to the last three questions: _____ (J-6)

• Finally, add the totals from all six groups of questions and place that score below: (J-1) plus (J-2) plus (J-3) plus (J-4) plus (J-5) plus (J-6):

Total score for all six groups of job/career questions: _____

This score can help you to make your decision, based on the evaluation procedures described below.

A Note about Your Options For Quitting or Staying in a Job
In the next chapter, I'll discuss in some detail six options you have for quitting or staying:

• *Quitting immediately.*

• *Resigning with the intention of a delayed quit.*

• *Announcing your intention to quit without stating any conditions.*

• *Announcing your intention to quit with conditions necessary for staying.*

- *Staying with a totally different approach to your situation.*

- *Staying and bringing about change in the situation.*

The six options are mentioned here only in relation to evaluating your scores. Your results will accentuate certain options; you can read more about those options in the next chapter.

While each personal circumstance is unique, the following section offers guidelines for evaluating your score.

Evaluating Your Scores for Job and Career Questions

With a total between 0 and 7, your job or career appears to have a high amount of potential left in it for you. At least you seem to feel good about the possibilities. The following options would be best for you to explore if you are still uncertain:

- *Staying with a totally different approach to your situation.*

- *Staying and bringing about change in the situation.*

If you scored 0 to 7 and are still confused, consider this option:

- *Announcing your intention to quit with conditions necessary for staying.*

However, if you scored that low — especially with a score below 5 — and still are not happy, you may have a deeper conflict which you might want to consider exploring with a professional counselor. (Please do not think this relates to weakness or that you have a batch of problems. Seeking help is always an act of strength if it moves you from confusion to clarity.)

With a total of 8 to 15, you might want to consider the following options:

- *Announcing your intention to quit without stating any conditions.*

- *Announcing your intention to quit with conditions necessary for staying.*

- *Staying with a totally different approach to your situation.*

These scores, while not "scientific," do represent your feelings about your job or career. Scoring 8 to 15 indicates — based on your assessment of the situation — that there is some potential room to work. If the score is 10 or less, or if you feel good about the potential for change in your situation, you might want to consider the following option:

- *Staying and bringing about change in the situation.*

With a total of 16 to 25, one reality is evident: you really do not see high hopes in your job or career circumstances. From your perspective — the way you answered the questions — it does not appear that there is great opportunity for finding meaning and fulfillment in your work.

With a score in this range, you might want to consider the following options:

- *Resigning with the intention of a delayed quit.*

- *Announcing your intention to quit without stating any conditions.*

- *Announcing your intention to quit with conditions necessary for staying.*

Because you are unique and the decision you make is going to have important consequences for you, I want to emphasize that what follows is my opinion. It is a very strong opinion; however, it is stated to guide you rather than to influence you to subscribe to my belief.

Any score more than 25 is not worthy of anyone. You have the brainpower and the resources to find better in your life — no matter how down-trodden you might feel now. A score of more than 25 indicates your circumstances could be adversely affecting your personal well-being.

If you scored more than 25, consider the following options:

- *Quitting immediately.*

- *Resigning with the intention of a delayed quit.*

- *Announcing your intention to quit without stating any conditions.*

- *Announcing your intention to quit with conditions necessary for staying.*

A score of more than 25 suggests quitting may be necessary — especially if the potential for change doesn't exist.

(Even 16 - 25 should be tolerated only as a temporary condition which is going to improve.)

The priorities are yours. They guide your life and in the long run make it meaningful or rob it of meaning. If the questions and resulting scores have helped you to clarify your priorities, then you have been well served.

Case Study: George and His Multi-Level Marketing Nightmare

George refers to himself as a "junkie to multi-level marketing" in the same manner that an alchoholic points to drink as his or her potential downfall. In on the ground floor of a "wonderful money-making opportunity," George rose quickly in the superstructure of a fast-growing health product business.

Working fourteen to sixteen hours a day, George had more than 400 people in his downline (sales reps from whom he derived a commission) within eight months. However, something was beginning to gnaw at George: he knew that most of the people in his downline couldn't care less about health or the products they were buying. They simply wanted to get rich.

George completed the "Knowing When to Quit Index" and got a score of 18.

George knew he was miserable, but he was making more than $6000 a month; within a few months that monthly figure would top $20,000. However, George also sensed the high personal cost: he was feeling more and more stress in his job, and enjoying it less and less.

He set up a meeting in Phoenix to recruit more people — people who would get him closer to that $20,000-a-month goal. A critical event happened at that meeting which added to his misery: one of the people who tasted a product had a severe allergic reaction and was taken away in an ambulance. George began hearing rumors of similar incidents all across the country.

I asked George to score himself on the Index again. This time he scored 27.

That was it! George decided his personal welfare was worth more than any monthly figure and pulled out. So did the company; six weeks later it went bankrupt.

The Knowing When to Quit Index for Relationships and Marriage

The following steps provide a procedure for combining your scores for the question sets you answered in Chapters 4 - 7. If you work your way through this process, you'll have a rough total "score," which may help you to see more objectively how strong your feelings really are about your relationship situation.

• Go back to page 39 in Chapter 4 and find your total for the questions you answered "yes." Write that number — Total "R-1" — in the space below:

Total for relationship questions from Chapter 4: _____ (R-1)

• Now go back to page 46 in Chapter 5 and find your total of questions answered "yes." Place that number (R-2) in the space below:

Total for relationship questions from Chapter 5: _____ (R-2)

• Go back to page 55 in Chapter 6 and find the total (R-3) of questions you answered "no." Write that number below. (Note: in the previous two groups, you totalled your "YES's" In this group — and only this group — you are totalling your "NO's.")

Total for relationship questions in Chapter 6: _____ (R-3)

• Go to page 65 in Chapter 7 and find the total (R-4) of questions you *left blank*. Write that total in the space below. (Note: In the other question groups, you totalled the items you marked "X." In this group — and only this group — you are totalling the items you *left blank*.)

Total nourishing relationship questions left blank
in Chapter 7: _____ (R-4)

• Also in Chapter 7 you answered questions about how toxic your environment was. Please go to page 66 and find the total (R-5) of times you answered yes; write your "R-5" total in the space below.

Total for toxic relationship questions from Chapter 7:

_____(R-5)

• For the six questions below, place an X next to those which are true for you. These are new questions; you have not answered them before.

_____ 1. I really do not feel any better about my marriage or relationship since I have been reading reading this book.

_____ 2. As much as I have looked for light at the end of the tunnel, I really don't see any.

_____ 3. I firmly believe there is much more potential for my life outside of this marriage or relationship.

_____ 4. I do not sense my partner has the commitment or motivation to make our marriage or relationship work.

_____ 5. I believe that I have much more of a chance for happiness if I am away from my partner.

_____ 6. I do not believe there is any chance to change anything for the better in our marriage or relationship.

Total of X's for the six questions above: _____ (R-6)

• Finally, add the totals from all six *groups* of questions and place that score below: (R-1) plus (R-2) plus (R-3) plus (R-4) plus (R-5) plus (R-6).

Total score for all six groups of questions: _____

This score can help you to make your decision, based on the evaluation procedures described below.

A Note About Your Options for Quitting or Staying in a Relationship

In the next chapter, I'll discuss in some detail six options you have for quitting or staying:

- *Quitting immediately.*

- *Resigning with the intention of a delayed quit.**

- *Announcing your intention to quit without stating any conditions.*

- *Announcing your intention to quit with conditions necessary for staying.*

- *Staying with a totally different approach to your situation.*

- *Staying and bringing about change in the situation.*

The six options are mentioned now only in relation to evaluating your scores. Your results will accentuate certain options, then you can read more about those options in the next chapter.

* (*Resigning with the intention of a delayed quit* will not be used as an option here since it has merit only in the workplace.)

While each personal circumstance is unique, the following section offers some guidelines for evaluating your score.

Evaluating Your Score for Relationship Questions

With a total between 0 and 7, your marriage or relationship appears still to have high potential for you. At least you seem to feel good about the possibilities. The following options would be best for you to explore:

- *Staying with a totally different approach to your situation.*

- *Staying and bringing about change in the situation.*

If you scored 0 to 7 and are still confused, consider this option:

- *Announcing your intention to quit with conditions necessary for staying.*

However, if you scored that low — especially with a score below 5 — and still are not happy, you may have a deeper conflict which you might want to consider exploring with a professional counselor. (Please do not think this relates to weakness or that you have a batch of problems. Seeking help is always an act of strength if it moves you from confusion to clarity.)

With a total of 8 to 15, you might want to consider the following options:

- *Announcing your intention to quit without stating any conditions.*

- *Announcing your intention to quit with conditions necessary for staying.*

- *Staying with a totally different approach to your situation.*

Scoring 8 to 15 indicates — based on your assessment of the situation — that there is some potential room to work. If the score is 10 or less, or if you feel good about the potential for change in your situation, you might want to consider the following option:

- *Staying and bringing about change in the situation.*

With a total of 16 to 25, one reality is evident: you really do not see high hopes in your marriage or relationship. From your perspective — the way you answered the questions — it does not appear that there is great opportunity for finding the nourishment and opportunities for mutual love which you seek.

With a score in this range, you might want to consider the following options:

- *Announcing your intention to quit without stating any conditions.*

- *Announcing your intention to quit with conditions necessary for staying.*

Because you are unique and the decision you make is going to have important consequences for you, I want to emphasize that what follows is my opinion. It is a very strong opinion; however, it is stated to guide you rather than to influence you to subscribe to my belief.

Any score more than 25 is not worthy of a relationship or marriage. Two people in love should be able to find something much better than what such high scores indicate. Unlike a score for a job or career, however, the upside potential is better — particularly if you have a partner who truly wants to do his or her part to improve the relationship.

If you scored more than 25, consider the following options:

- *Quitting immediately*.

- *Announcing your intention to quit without stating any conditions*.

- *Announcing your intention to quit with conditions necessary for staying*.

A score of more than 25 suggests quitting may be necessary, especially if the potential — or your partner's willingness — for change doesn't exist.

Even 16 - 25 should be tolerated only as a temporary condition which is going to improve.

The priorities are yours. They guide your life and in the long run make it meaningful or rob it of meaning. If the questions and resulting scores have helped you to clarify your priorities, you have been well served.

Case Study: Noreen and David's Positive Form of Quitting

For the past few years of Noreen and David's marriage, Noreen's discontent had increased. She married David immediately upon graduating from college and became pregnant with her first child in less than a year. Now, ten years into the marriage, she was feeling the need to get out — to breathe again.

David didn't take any of this seriously. He was a stock broker whose skill and knowledge allowed him to be dented only slightly with October 1987's "Black Monday." David brought home a very comfortable six-figure income, and all that he really expected of Noreen was to entertain, take care of the children, and maintain their large house — along with being a "good wife," of course. For Noreen that was too much... and not enough. Taking care of three children, maintaining a large house, and entertaining for a rapidly increasing number of David's clients had become an intolerable burden for her. She wanted more challenge in her life, and more time away from "motherly" and "wifely" duties.

David, of course, didn't want to lose his "good deal," and said, "No way!" At my suggestion, Noreen went through all the questions of the "Knowing When to Quit Index." She was shocked to find a score of 22. She realized that her environment was no longer nourishing or supporting. When she asked David to do the "Knowing When to Quit Index," he was at first resistant. Finally he agreed. He scored 10! The contrast in their scores brought their differences into sharp focus. Noreen told David: "You have a good deal; I don't. Either I find happiness in this marriage, or I'm leaving it."

After recovering from Noreen's atypical assertiveness, David agreed to discuss the matter. Noreen admitted that she didn't want to quit the marriage but saw no other alternative if they didn't quit many of the patterns which had led to her unhappiness.

It took weeks of negotiations, but Noreen and David did not quit their marriage. Instead, they quit the beliefs and patterns which had not served their marriage well. David used some of his six-figure income to hire a maid and someone to care for the children from time to time. Noreen agreed that entertaining was essential to David's career, but they worked out ways to get more mileage out of fewer engagements. Noreen began taking classes at the local community college to begin a career of her own.

Both took the "Knowing When to Quit Index" six months after their first time; this time both scored near ten (David was still a few points lower, of course!). They did not have to quit their marriage; they only needed to quit the behaviors and faulty ideas which were blocking their individual fulfillment in the relationship.

So What Does It All Mean?

Your score on the "Knowing When to Quit Index" — job or relationship — is meant only to be a guideline. It has value to the degree that it touches something inside of you. Strong feelings are much better indicators than raw scores!

I have talked about "inner messages" throughout this book. I hope the Index has helped you gain sharper inner clarity, and moved you closer to making the best decision for your life. The next chapter takes a closer look at six options for "where you go from here."

Still Confused?

If you are still confused, you have a number of alternatives:

- You can burn this book, throw it away, or return it to the library.

- You can get your mind off your situation for a few days, then answer the Index questions again.

- You can begin now to re-read pertinent parts of the book, then answer the index questions again.

The first alternative does little for you, but could help me and my publisher — should you later decide to buy another copy of the book!

The other alternatives can give you an idea where your feelings are heading. By going through the questions again over a number of days or weeks, you may sense your feelings heading in a certain direction; you don't have to limit yourself to one set of data. While your first scores may be — as is often the case — amazingly accurate, testing again can help you to separate your own feelings from the attitudes and ideas you've absorbed from other people.

Be sure to use your journal/log regularly during this period of decision-making. Read back over your earlier notes, and make complete notes about your feelings as you score your "Knowing When to Quit Index." Let your log be both an adjunct to your memory and a guide to your next steps, as patterns and clear feelings emerge.

Ready to move on to *action*?

Action

Chapter 13.

Your Six Choices for Movement

You now stand at a crossroad. First, you analyzed yourself. Then, you explored your social environment. Finally, you moved yourself to exploring your best decision. Now you are ready to explore action. You have six options:

- *Quitting immediately.*
- *Resigning with the intention of a delayed quit.*
- *Announcing your intention to quit without stating any conditions.*
- *Announcing your intention to quit with conditions necessary for staying.*
- *Staying with a totally different approach to your situation.*
- *Staying and bringing about change in the situation.*

In 1972 I was tired of teaching. I had been teaching mainly freshman composition, and was quickly growing weary of having to teach basic grammar even to the most advanced composition classes. At that time, quitting was out of the question. I was in a highly nourishing and stimulating environment. Thus, I began searching for different ways to approach my job.

The previous summer I had seen an effective slide-tape presentation at a summer camp program. Amazed what could be done with slides and music, I started making slide-tape presentations to stimulate writing. This created excitement for both me and my students.

Eventually, I realized that it was possible to demonstrate certain writing skills visually. A beginning paragraph could be demonstrated by having the music and the pictures proceed from the general to the specific. Furthermore, I also was able to visually demonstrate transition, parallel structure, and comparison-contrast. Within three years, a profession which had begun to bore me had become very exciting.

Eventually, I received invitations to speak at eight teachers' conventions so that I could demonstrate my approach. This sharing of something exciting gave even greater meaning to my work. During the next six years, I looked forward to going to class. I eventually created thirty-three slide-tape presentations.

The lesson to be learned in this example is: *be absolutely sure that your job is dead before you kill it*.

I finally killed that job in 1980 because there were no more hills to conquer. This time, I could not find a way out of my boredom. Thus, I changed careers.

Before *you* make a major change, let's take a look at those six options.

Quitting Immediately
Rarely is the immediate quit a good idea. It works best in highly catastrophic relationships among single people. High toxicity or constant turmoil may necessitate a quick exit.

Yet, even in relationships among single people, the immediate quit is rarely the best move. Quitting is more effective and compassionate after some communication.

In the workplace, the immediate quit can be professional suicide. An immediate quit may feel good... for about twenty-four hours. Eventually, concerns about a damaged future emerge. Immediate quits make for dramatic conversation; however, in the job market they rarely produce good results.

Very few people go through with an immediate quit. Those who do have been pushed to the limit (at least that's the way they feel). Usually, it's a straw-that-broke-the-camel's-back incident.

Larry Brown, coach of the 1988 NCAA champion University of Kansas Jayhawks basketball team, publicly admitted that he had left too soon as head coach at UCLA (earlier in his career). In retrospect, he concluded that, even though he didn't have an easy time, the worst was behind him. He acknowledged that he would have had the support he needed to build a good program at UCLA, had he stayed longer. (As I wrote this, UCLA was interviewing Brown for a possible return to Westwood. As it turned out Kansas made it worth his while to stay in Lawrence.)

My friends Walter and Paul both left teaching after their first year beacuse their experiences had been so miserable. I pleaded with them to try teaching again *at another school*. However, they were so bruised that they wanted to leave the profession — and the bad memories. The students had loved both of these first-year teachers, and considered them effective. I believe that these men — because of their love for kids and for their respective subjects — could have found fulfillment as teachers — in a more nourishing atmosphere.

Resigning With The Intention of a Delayed Quit

This comes closest to an immediate quit. Yet, it allows

those left behind some dignity. The resignation with a time delay before the quit indicates both that you are willing to allow a time of transition, and that you are firm in your decision to quit.

While this alternative shows both courtesy and compassion in the workplace, it rarely works in marriage and relationships. Many have mentioned that once they knew it was over, they wished they had parted sooner.

After announcing their intention to leave a relationship or marriage, some partners stay for a long time, thinking this is noble. It isn't. It only gives false hope.

In the workplace, there is another concern. After you announce your intention to quit, you will be more relaxed. With less stress, you could enjoy your job more, tempting you to believe that you've made a mistake. While this is a very human reaction, it is rarely correct. You made your decision under normal conditions. Now that you are leaving, your situation is no longer normal.

The other pitfall is not as frequent, however, it can produce needless anxiety. Sometimes your circumstances actually do get better. This could confuse you. I got unusually good treatment after announcing my intention to quit a teaching job. I was the fourth person to resign during the first eleven weeks of school. Yet I didn't realize that until later. (In fact, I later found out that I was the second person to announce my resignation *that day*!) Because I was the first person to resign without an immediate quit, my superiors had a better feeling about me and were unusually nice. While that situation got a whole lot better, it never got good.

Announcing Your Intention to Quit Without Stating Any Conditions

You can approach this option two ways. First, you can state your hope that the situation will get better. That means you aren't putting any limitations on your experience. It also means that you aren't offering any specific guidelines as to how or why you might remain. You will trust your own perception as to whether circumstances improve enough to merit remaining. You have no specific expectations. You don't state any because you may not yet be sure what they are.

This is not being a prima donna. It is an affirmation of your right to enjoy your environment and use your skills as effectively as possible.

Another approach to this option involves specific expectations, however, you do not state them. You know what you want, but you keep it yourself. For the person who wants to be absolutely sure no one will behave unusually or be overly nice in an attempt to manipulate, this approach is best.

You want to avoid the appearance of being manipulative, however. By its very nature, an announced resignation with a future decision pending can appear manipulative. Stating that you are seeking clarity instead of attention will put many minds to rest.

In relationships and marriage, the announcement of an intent to quit will have a much greater impact. Unlike a work-related announcement, this may come as more of a shock than you might expect. That's the bad news.

The good news is that for the most part you have only one partner to inform. Of course, there may also be children, and your parents, in-laws and other relatives must be told eventually. Jobs rarely last forever, but intimate relationships come under an umbrella of higher expectation.

In unstable relationships the announcement of an intent to end the relationship will actually hasten its end. This rarely happens where there is some hope, however. If there is potential for healing, the announcement of an intended quit will usually stimulate necessary action and communication. If the relationship is beyond hope, the announcement of an intended quit will only intensify the block to communication.

Your partner might say, "If you feel that way, let's end it right now." If that's your partner's best shot, you are being helped more than you realize. This indicates little or no potential for communication. In fact, this lack of communication is probably one of your main reasons for making the announcement.

In the workplace we tend to fear any negative response to an announcement. Despite all our fears, negative responses are rare. The announcement of an intention to quit simply does not turn out to be as threatening as we might have imagined. (That in itself can be damaging to some egos.) Employers are paid to deal with this, and they have dealt with it before.

Be prepared to be bumped into another option. If you are making no demands with your announcement, you might be asked to make some so that others have a chance to improve what concerns you. Even if you choose at first not to announce any conditions, you should at least be ready so you can give them if asked. If you have no ideas for improvement if asked, it will appear as if you haven't given the matter much thought.

Be sure that you understand the difference between specific and general demands. Of the following two statements, the latter more specific example is more effective:

I want things to be different around here. I'm tired of being treated like I'm not important. I've done a lot for this company and what do I have to show for it? I still think that I'm being grossly underpaid.

Here are some changes which I think are essential. First of all, I would like to be given tasks that more effectively reflect my mathematical training. Since coming here I have helped increase productivity by 32 percent in my department. Yet in the last three years my salary has only increased 16 percent.

When Marv asked Claudia to marry him, Claudia considered this the best time to tell him that something didn't feel right about the relationship, and that she was thinking of ending it. When a shocked Marv asked why, Claudia could not put her finger on any specific reasons. She knew only that she needed to feel much better about the relationship before making a marriage commitment.

Claudia's friends told her she was a "flake." Claudia countered with, "I know when something feels good, and I know when something doesn't feel good, but I don't always know the reasons why. If I don't feel better about this relationship in a couple of months, I'm going to get out of it."

Two months later, Claudia's feelings had grown even worse, and she broke up with Marv. A few months after that, mutual friends told Claudia that Marv had deep-seated emotional problems which he wouldn't even admit to himself; evidently other relationships had collapsed for him for the same reasons. Claudia was glad that she trusted her gut feelings, even thought there were few things — at the time — that she could specifically spot.

Announcing Your Intention to Quit With Conditions for Staying

In some circumstances this strategy can so change a working situation that it will merit your remaining. However, in others your announcement could appear to change things for the worse. (This will not happen in a job environment which is good for you.)

There is only one solid reason for an announcement of an intended quit with conditions stated for staying: you need to see the potential for change before making your final decision. Unlike the announcement with no stated conditions, you allow others to participate in the necessary change. There is nothing wrong with boldly stating what it will take to keep you in your job.

If you feel this is rocking the boat, simply remind yourself that it is not your intention to *sink* the boat. You want to rock just enough to see if anyone feels that you are worth saving. With this option be prepared for the worst. If being told to look elsewhere for a job is something you can't handle, this is not your option! Here are some of the worst things that could happen:

You could be fired on the spot.

You could be told by your employer that you are the most unrealistic jerk who ever worked there.

Psychotherapy could be highly recommended.

You could be told to put your expectations in a place which is physically impossible.

As potentially traumatic as each is, the chance of any of them happening is very rare.

It's not hard to get a reputation for being demanding. Some people get that just by asking for what they deserve. In your situation you will be asking for what you feel you deserve. In the quiet of your own thinking, you have determined that your circumstances do not merit staying. You have gone further than most people in assessing what it will take to keep you. There is no reason why you should ask for this with your head hung low.

Russ was a middle-level manager with an emerging high-tech company. He had advanced quickly into management on the strength of his excellent creative efforts in computer program design. Administrative duties were placing an increasing burden on his time, until he announced that he was going to quit if he couldn't return to creating new software — his first love.

Jim, Russ's very aware boss, realized that he would rather have Russ back in programming than lose him altogether. Jim saw a way out which might work for both of them:

Russ, I really need you as a supervisor of programmers. Yet, I recognize that you still want to create programs yourself. Why don't we work it that you spend half your time creating programs and the other half supervising? You can help me select one of the other programmers to assist you with the supervision. That way, we'll have two opinions. Can your ego handle that one?

Russ realized his happiness at work depended on having his ego handle it. He agreed to a slight reduction in salary and went back to doing what he really loved, while retaining his mid-manager status. His request for a specific change led to a compromise which met the needs of his company and still gave Russ what he really wanted.

Staying With a Completely Different Approach to Your Situation

The following conditions should be present if this option is going to work best for you:

You like the people you are working with.

The people you work for respect you and allow you appropriate freedom.

Your working environment is at least minimally nourishing.

It would be tragic if a potential treasure lay within your own job and you left it prematurely. You owe it to yourself to explore this possibility.

Many interesting things have happened as a result of searching for another approach to work:

A very bored personnel manager found more meaning in his work when he volunteered to counsel with people who were having problems with their work. Instead of working mainly to bring new people in, he now found a challenge in helping the disgruntled to stay. Without this new meaning he would not have felt like staying himself.

A nurse was bored with her twelve-year job until she began to study stress management techniques. She became inspired to make herself an expert. At first, she just relieved her own stress. Then she found more meaning in her job as she helped her patients relieve their own stress. Eventually she became in instructor for her fellow nurses, and this added even more meaning to her job.

In each case, the outer job remained the same. The difference was in the individual approach. Even if you strongly feel that you must leave your job, you will have greater peace of mind if you have sought alternatives within your job.

Staying and Bringing About Change In the Situation

While this and the previous option overlap somewhat, their main thrusts are different. In the previous option, it is mainly you who must change. With this option, it is mainly the situation which must change.

Betty, the secretary we met in Chapter 10, did not find meaning in her work until she volunteered to help with increasing the productivity in her office. A smart boss eventually realized that she had to be more involved and help to create change if she were going to stay. She not only stayed, she also became so effective that she was promoted.

She found much more fulfillment making her situation better than she would have found in starting over at a new place.

This is the "light at the end of the tunnel" option. Through your exploration and communication, you realize that change is possible and that this change has the potential of re-establishing a nourishing and/or challenging environment.

Often the very act of bringing about the change can be highly rewarding and can breathe new vitality into a job or relationship.

John and Tanya's marriage appeared doomed. John was not even hiding the fact that he was sleeping with other women. Tanya was just as open about her lack of sexual desire for John — or any other man, for that matter. Both sought counseling mainly to justify ending the marriage. However, they encountered a counselor who helped them focus more on healing than on ending. The counselor met with both of them individually for a few sessions at first, then brought them together. "While ending your marriage is always an option, I'd like both of you to consider if there is any way you can stay together and have both of you win," the counselor said.

John and Tanya realized that they had been focusing more on losing than winning. Tanya felt that John was too obsessed with the trucking business he owned, and, of course, she was not happy about John's cheating.

With help from the counselor, John realized his cheating stemmed mainly from, as he saw it, a "noble gesture." Raised to believe that any form of oral sex was "dirty," John sought oral experiences only with other women. Since Tanya did not have this conditioning, John realized that the problem resulted mainly from lack of communication. John also realized that his string of affairs with much younger women came more from his concern about 'getting older" than anything to do with Tanya. He made a commitment to deal with this further in therapy.

Within a few sessions both realized that their marriage had a lot of potential left in it. Tanya accepted that she had not kept herself up and found new excitement in losing twenty pounds and dressing better. John agreed to stop the affairs with other women and to cut back on the excessive time he spent at his business. Both were willing to change, and this helped them save their marriage.

Within the workplace many options can be explored before making a decision to quit. Changes in recent years have introduced more team approaches to work, with staff and management working together to bring about change, and enlightened management asking for active participation by workers in arriving at key decisions. More and more companies realize that increased productivity comes mainly from increased morale. In-house programs and outside consulting aid in creating a more nourishing — and productive — work atmosphere. Your expression of discontent could be the motivating force for such action. You owe it to yourself to see if anyone will listen. Moreover, no one can listen if you don't say anything!

Dianne works for one of the major airlines as a reservation clerk. She seriously considered quitting her job because of the high stress levels which resulted from having her calls monitored by a supervisor and having computers keep track of how much time was spent on each call. "If you go over 109 seconds, they give you a bad mark. If more than eleven seconds elapse between calls, we also get bad marks. What used to be a very happy office is now very tense."

When Dianne mentioned she was going to quit, she found the upper management willing to listen. They asked her what it would take for her to remain. Dianne said she wanted to involve the other workers, and began surveying them. Everyone agreed that managers need to know how their people are coming across to the public. Almost every worker, however, felt the stress came from not knowing when they were going to be monitored. They also wanted the freedom to decide when 109 seconds was too short a time to get the job done.

Upper management agreed to tell workers when they were going to be monitored. They also dropped the ''109 seconds'' demand, yet urged that the reservation clerks make efficient use of their time and still have their times recorded. While all the problems aren't solved, morale and communication have improved enough for Diane to remain. For her efforts, her fellow workers appointed her as their official representative.

****

Consider which of the six options would work best for you. Once you have made your decision, the next chapter will help you build a bridge to what's next in your life.

Chapter 14.

Building the Bridge

If you have decided to quit, building a bridge to your new life is essential, and will increase the peace of mind needed to follow through on your decision. If you are still undecided, the process of beginning to build a bridge will significantly enhance your clarity.

Either way, you will increase your mental efficiency and reduce your level of anxiety. The better you are at building a bridge to what's next, the higher your chances for success.

"Bridges," incidentally, do not focus only on the workplace; in a unique manner, this process also applies to relationships and marriage.

Some people feel good about making a leap. It is cathartic and leaves a clean and released feeling... for a day or two. In the workplace this approach works best if:

1. You are in a job so menial that finding another job like it is no problem.
2. You are working in a job which pays minimum wage, and you live in an area where getting another minimum wage job will not be difficult.

3. You have enough money to cover yourself and your family for six months and can use most of that money for an effective job search.
4. You have a standing offer of another job.
5. You are independently wealthy and don't need to work.

Building the Bridge in the Workplace

In the workplace the circumstances are usually much more complicated. However, they are also usually much less painful. As much as you might want to believe otherwise, you are going to be more easily replaced in the workplace. Another employee can be found quickly.

• The first move you can make is to *read. Books about the marketplace, your job, or a potential new career* will be quite helpful. Even if you acquire little useful information at the start, you are at least beginning to develop a mental set. This can be more valuable than you may realize. A naive mental set versus a knowledgable one shows up quite obviously in interviews, applications, and exploratory letters.

I highly recommend a bookstore or library visit. Simply browsing through books can give you an idea of the range of directions in which you can move. Many valuable books exist on shifting careers, interviewing skills, writing resumes, alternative jobstyles, job possibilities, ways to dress for interviewing and career advancement, and many other related topics. You will find many other options as you browse.

• Many colleges and universities, some community mental health centers, and most public employment offices offer *information banks, job listings,* and *career counseling workshops*. Seek out the resources available in your community.

• Another area which can be a great help is an *employment agency*. They usually make no charge until they find you a job. (Then they fleece you royally!) There, you can find information about job opportunities, and whether another geographic area might be best in your field of interest. You can also gain information on other jobs in your career field.

• The fourth area of building a bridge is actually *filling out applications*. Sometimes this can so drive you crazy that you might reconsider your decision to quit. Most applications are tedious and ask for unnecessary and superfluous information. (As Dante had his special place in Hell for traitors, I hold the same for those who dream up applications!)

That's the bad news about filling out applications.

The good news is that you are given a wonderful opportunity to clarify your values. You can sharpen your written communication skills, as you learn exactly what a potential future employer might want.

• In bridge-building it is essential to give yourself the edge. As ridiculous as it sounds, I urge you to *practice interviewing* where you have little or no chance of getting the job. Don't be afraid to drop in unnannounced and ask if you can speak to the personnel manager. (The two best jobs I ever received resulted from dropping in unannounced. In each I figured that I didn't have a chance. I was probably so relaxed that I made the right impression!) Some personnel managers find this impressive. Others find it an intrusion. If you are just practicing, it doesn't matter (unless you are in a community so small that you'd be in danger of developing a "reputation"!).

• As your confidence increases, you will get an idea of when you will want to *do serious interviewing*. Now you are at that final phase of bridge-building. You can go to those interviews which offer jobs which you want. You'll be more comfortable and confident as you negotiate for the right to have that job. (Whether you realize it or not, "negotiation" is exactly what what you are doing in an interview.)

If you have learned your job-seeking and interviewing skills well, you have that "significant edge." You'll have a big advantage in gaining a good job no matter how weak the market is.

And speaking of weak markets, be sure you have thoroughly explored the potential for jobs in your field (and in places in which you are willing to live) *before* you quit. As much as I favor going with your feelings in leaving a dead-end job, I recognize that in hard times one can spend a lot of time pounding the streets by leaving one job before another is on your hook!

Resign Yourself!

Whether you have made a firm decision to quit or are still considering your options, I recommend the following as a very powerful exercise:

Write a letter of resignation, but DO NOT send it. Writing a letter now will help you crystallize your feelings. Even if you have made the decision *not* to quit, I still urge you to write such a letter. If no blocked feelings come up, you're fairly sure your decision to stay is a good one.

If you are planning to end a relationship or marriage, you might wonder if a letter of "resignation" is appropriate. Remember, at this point you are only trying to crystallize your ideas. The very act of writing the letter (knowing you'll not be sending it) will help you gain clarification of your own feelings which you couldn't get from direct communication with your partner.

Don't worry about grammar, spelling, or syntax. All you need to do is sit down and write. This particular letter is for you only.

Here are a couple of examples:

Dear Henry,
When I first met you, you were my knight in shining armor. I think I might have done you a disservice by

expecting so much of you. Now I realize that you are one of the supreme jerks of my whole life. My hope that you would grow up and become more mature in your approach was a false hope. You just don't have it, and I am tired of seeing a baby come home every night and whine about how badly the world is treating him...

Dear Mr. Scrooge:
One of the most essential points of leadership for a good manager is to recognize good people, and allow those people to participate in the growth and success of the working situation. Even mediocre managers have some of these skills. However, this is an area where you possess total myopia. your insecurity and inability to lead have blocked any possible fulfillment from creeping into my job. Therefore, it is my intention to get the *&%$ out of this job, and allow some other masochist to try his hand at it...

Remember, this is a letter to explore your own feelings. You can pull out all the stops, since you'll probably burn it!

Prepare Yourself for Arguments
In building your bridge, you want to be prepared for any attempts to dissuade you from doing what's best for you. Such preparation will give you greater confidence, and make your transition much easier.

If you have concluded that your situation merits quitting, you will want to gather your clearest explanations and practice saying them in ways others can understand. You will always perform best if you have prepared your ideas in advance. Preparing solid, specific reasons for your decision can give you a confident feeling. Moreover, the better you prepare, the more good reasons you might find for quitting. Your very preparation might actually unveil good reasons for your decision.

Building the Bridge in Relationships and Marriage

It amazes me how many relationships needlessly end "cold turkey." A toxic argument or the discovery of infidelity sparks a quick end. Relationships which end in the heat of the moment avoid that most important element of healing — forgiveness. Television has done an excellent job of conditioning us for the dramatic exit. Sometimes in real life, the parting lines are almost word-for-word from a soap opera.

If the cold-turkey ending spells a potential disaster for short-term relationships, it spells even greater disaster for longer relationships and marriages. I have a friend who is ending his six-year marriage as a result of one very toxic argument. He has it set in his mind that there can be no reconciliation. In the time it took to pack, he was gone.

While this "drama" might feel good for the moment, he will have to deal with his wife and two expensive lawyers. Building a bridge might have made that process smoother — perhaps even unnecessary.

Whether ending a relationship or a marriage, there are certain things you can do to build a bridge. Many of these represent mental efforts. However, they aid transition and reduce anxiety. A bridge may not stop the pain, but it can ease it.

• I highly recommend that people who are considering leaving a marriage *read books about divorce*. While the advice varies widely and some may not work for you, they do describe situations which you are going to face. They also give you mental preparation for circumstances which you may not have thought about. They can help prevent a lot of surprises. Reading case histories will help give you confidence that you eventually are going to feel better. Since divorce breaks down into stages, an advance understanding of these stages is helpful.

• Exiting a marriage or other relationship, it might be helpful to *read books about single life*. Most books about the single life are highly idealistic, and generally lack the professionalism of books about divorce. Whereas a majority of the divorce books are written by psychologists and social workers, books about single life tend to be written by non-professionals who are single. Nevertheless, they can — if you read selectively — help to clarify what you may expect.

• The older you are, the more you might want to find out about *singles groups*. Some of them are very good and provide an excellent transition for the recently-divorced (or recently-detached). Each singles group has its own personality. Some are "lonely hearts" groups. Some are "meat markets." Others center on discussions and helping people to know one another by talking about certain subjects. In this building-the-bridge stage, I have found that most people use singles groups as a clearing house. There they exchange information on the best places to meet people. Those most interested in the "best singles bar" can find out about one which will meet their needs. Similarly, one can find out about the best bookstores, churches, health clubs, civic groups, and other resources for meeting people.

• For the person entering the singles scene once again, I recommend *video dating services*. Contrary to their image, they are not lonely hearts services, nor do they attract those with the loser mentality like so many singles groups. A person has to have a fairly high self-esteem to be interviewed and then have that interview seen by many others. I have found people to be enthusiastic about video dating for a number of reasons: you know for sure that the person you are watching wants to meet other people; you are protected from people you don't want to date (your name and number are not given out unless both of you agree to a match); you can meet a lot of people more quickly; the humiliation of the singles bar scene is eliminated.

For people who have been in long relationships or marriages, entry into the world of dating can be nothing short of traumatic. Video dating services provide an ease in transition. If you feel that you might become quickly overloaded (as many do), you can put yourself on hold and give yourself more time to breathe by making your file inactive for a while.

• *Take your time*. Allowing yourself some time to breathe can be very helpful. Going out with different people after being exclusively with one person can be quite an adjustment. The insecurity about what to do about sex and other dating "demands" can drain one to the point of exhaustion. If you think you might be one of these people, I urge you to treat yourself gently and ease the transition by beginning slowly to build a bridge. No rule says you have to begin dating again immediately.

Should you get into the singles scene once again, you will find that there are two ways to experience loneliness: by yourself and by being with with a group of people. Many discover that the latter is a much more painful loneliness.

Incidentally, I have one firm rule relating to getting into another relationship quickly: DON'T! (unless your new relationship was the cause of the breakup of the first relationship).

• One final bit of advice for those coming off of long relationships and marriages: *The greatest skill you can acquire as a single person is to learn how to be comfortable with yourself*. The more you like being with yourself, the more you will attract the right person into your life.

Stuck on the Bridge?

Some folks will do all the self-analysis, social analysis, decision, and even action steps described in this book and still find it hard to move. This is human. It is also counter-productive. You've built your bridge with knowledge, care, and effectiveness. Yet, when it's time to move, the mover gets stuck in the middle of that bridge so carefully built.

Some find that they just cannot make this final move. The key word here is "final." The very finality of it creates anxiety and causes them to run for yet more advice. This is one time where running to others is not a good idea. The best move is to sit quietly and ask yourself if there really is any new pertinent information.

If you find yourself at this point, you may want to answer the self-analysis questions and score your "Knowing When to Quit Index" one more time.

If you are still experiencing a high degree of anxiety, you might consider one or two visits with a professional counselor, not because you are psychologically unbalanced but to regain your objectivity. The counselor's objective insight might be just the thing to help you understand why you are stuck. A counselor can help you see what your feelings really are. The cost for a couple of sessions could range between $50 and $200. At this critical point in your life, I urge you to find the best. If you are "stuck on the bridge," it could be the best money you have spent in years. Be sure to find someone who is an expert in career change or relationship counseling (depending upon your concern). Ask in advance about the counselor's procedures, training, experience, fees, and references.

Two Final Tidbits on Bridge-Building

The more comfortable you can become with remaining in your old job, the faster you will probably be offered a new one.

I cannot explain this. It comes under the realm of paradox. I have found my clients' experience supports this.

Part of your bridge-building could be to consciously develop
that kind of detachment. Be aware that this does not always
occur for those people who are seeking comfort and an escape
from their fears. It works wonderfully with those whose
comfort comes from inner strength to accept their situation
until they are able to change it.

*The less you try for a new situation, the less chance
you have of getting one.*

If you don't ask, you avoid rejection. That's the good
news.

The bad news is that you also avoid acceptance.

Chapter 15.

Leaving the Comfort of the Fire

In the time of primitive men and women, great joy came from the discovery of fire. Soon it became a ritual to sit around this new-found source of warmth and security. Before the discovery of fire, men and women explored boldly. They went deep into the caves, climbing high into the hills and seeking the source of streams. Searching diligently, they had opened new vistas, with abundant resources and natural wonders. Together they celebrated the joy of their discoveries.

But now they had fire.

The fire's comfort began to sap their power. Away from the fire they felt the contrasting cold. While the fire kept the beasts away, it also caused the darkness to be seen in darker contrast. Men and women quickly forgot how well they had handled the beasts before. As their fear of the beasts increased, they huddled around the fire for greater protection.

Where they once told tales of great explorers, they now described the horrors which lay beyond the fire. These stories made it even more appealing to sit around the fire. They may have had some truth; however, it didn't take long to equate venturing away from the fire with something horrible. The fact that this horror rarely happened was irrelevant.

Those who dared to move beyond the safety of the fire increasingly found themselves the objects of ridicule.

Thus, ridicule, stories, comfort, and fear soon kept ninety-percent huddled around the fire, despite ever-increasing boredom. Some may have despised being stuck in one place, but they could at least reassure themselves that they were warm.

There was, however, that rare soul who felt the push from within to move. Those who were so stirred knew that if they didn't keep moving and that if they got too comfortable, they would never explore again. Strengthened by the warmth of the day, they struck out from the warmth of the fire. They climbed high into the hills and gazed at unexplored vistas below. As the night brought its cold, they moved back to the fire's warmth. If they moved quickly, they could avoid both the cold and the ridicule.

Some became so fascinated with their explorations that they returned later and later to the fire. Those in charge made up punishments for failing to get back to the fire in time. For most, this dampened enthusiasm for further exploration. However, for those needing to explore further, this was taken as a sign. They did not understand the point of no return. To explore what they saw from high up on the hills, they knew they would have to cut themselves off from the rest of their community. The warmth of the fire had too great a price.

In the brightness of the sun these "outsiders" climbed to the top of the hill to get their bearings. Then they descended... on the other side. As they came down from the view, with the trees high above them, night began to fall. Almost immediately they felt the cold. To keep themselves on track in the increasing dark, they visualized the scenes they had seen from high on the hill. Gleaming silver rivers separated verdant valleys. Could they survive there, away from the warmth, ridicule, acceptance, ...and punishment which lay behind them?

While the primitive explorers may not have verbalized it, the comfort of the fire nearly kept them from walking through the night toward the gleaming silver river.

As the darkness filled the forest, the bold explorers felt the increasing cold, feared that they might freeze before they found the river, yet pressed on. Often through the night their fears were punctuated with thoughts of stupidity for leaving the fire. Yet something was stirring deep within. These cold and frightened early explorers *had* to make it to the gleaming silver river. Despite frightened and shivering bodies, they were warmed by the fire burning deep inside.

And that fire had to be tended.

Can You Be Happy If You Stay In This Job? (Chapter 4)

Place an X next to any of the questions to which you could answer "yes." Use your log to record your answers — and be sure to *date* your log entry.

_____ 1. Will my physical health be hurt by remaining?

_____ 2. Will my mental health be hurt by remaining?

_____ 3. Am I staying in these circumstances *mainly* because I have invested a lot of time in them?

_____ 4. Is the fear of what lies ahead adversely affecting my decision?

_____ 5. Am I experiencing an unusual lack of personal fulfillment?

_____ 6. Is it possible that I might be stuck (unable to move myself)?

_____ 7. Would I be relieved if I were removed from my situation?

_____ 8. Does my staying strongly indicate that I have become stagnant and/or afraid to move?

_____ 9. Am I remaining because I think I am "too busy" to look for something different?

_____ 10. Am I unhappy enough in this environment that it could be psychologically harmful?

_____ 11. Have I come to the point where there is no light at the end of the tunnel?

_____ 12. Has my situation eroded so slowly that I may not yet be aware how bad things really are?

Total _____ (J-1)

Will You Hurt Yourself By Remaining In Your Job? (Chapter 5)

Place an X next to any question in the following list to which your answer is "yes." Record your answers in your log.

_____ 1. Is this job causing significant harm to my mental or physical health?

_____ 2. Could I could gain more by quitting than staying?

_____ 3. Am I staying mainly because of economic security?

_____ 4. Am I stuck in a job which is doing me more harm than good?

_____ 5. Could I be staying in my work because it's predictable and I don't want to change?

_____ 6. Could I use my talents better in another job or career?

_____ 7. Am I staying because I don't want other people to think I'm selfish?

_____ 8. In the process of making my superiors winners, am I becoming a loser?

_____ 9. Am I afraid to admit to myself that this job is falling far short of my expectations?

_____ 10. Am I exhausted at the end of every working day?

_____ 11. Can I say that in relation to my job, the best days are behind me?

_____ 12. Would I be secretly relieved if I were removed from my job?

Total _____ (J-2)

Will You Hurt Others by Quitting Your Job or Career? (Chapter 6)

Place an X in the space next to each question you answer "no." (Note that you're checking NO's this time.) Record your answers in your log.

_____ 1. Will my quitting cause any harmful disruption?

_____ 2. Could I be underrating the harm that I might cause by quitting?

_____ 3. Will my company or place of employment be hurt significantly if I quit?

_____ 4. Is it possible that I'm remaining because I don't want to cause disturbance and hassle to certain people by leaving?

_____ 5. Would there be too many unusual physical disruptions (moving, etc.) to my family or friends?

_____ 6. Would it be too much of a financial adjustment for my family or friends if I quit?

_____ 7. Would my quitting necessitate my moving to another town?

_____ 8. If I am without income for a while, would this greatly hurt those I'm closest to?

_____ 9. Will I cause those closest to me to be embarrassed or humiliated if I quit?

Total _____ (J-3)

How Nourishing Is Your Job? (Chapter 7)

The following statements describe some features of a nourishing job. Remember to write down in your log any strong feelings which come up as you go through the list. Place an X next to those which apply.

_____ 1. You enjoy being with most of your co-workers.

_____ 2. You have the opportunity to use most of your training and talents.

_____ 3. You have the freedom to express what you are feeling.

_____ 4. You have praise and support from your superiors.

_____ 5. You feel that you are contributing something worthwhile.

_____ 6. The people around you give you the idea that what you are doing really matters.

Total X's _____ (N-J)   Total blanks _____ (J-4)

How Toxic Is Your Job?

The following descriptions will help you to determine if you are working in a toxic mental environment. Note any feelings as you explore the statements, and place an X next to any which apply to your job situation:

_____ 1. You experience more criticism than praise.

_____ 2. When people talk in groups, you hear mostly complaints.

_____ 3. You are constantly told that you are not doing enough.

_____ 4. You have bad relationships with many of your coworkers.

_____ 5. You are constantly told that you need to do better work.

_____ 6. You do not like what you are doing.

Total _____ (J-5)

RELATIONSHIP QUESTIONS

Can You Be Happy Staying in this Relationship? (Chapter 4)

In the list below, place an X next to any question you answer "yes." Note any feelings which emerge as you read the question. Trust those feelings and consider writing them down in your log as you experience them.

_____ 1. Will my physical health be hurt by remaining?

_____ 2. Will my mental health be hurt by remaining?

_____ 3. Am I staying in these circumstances mainly because I have invested a lot of time?

_____ 4. Am I inhibited to a point where I am not free to be myself?

_____ 5. Do I enjoy being with my partner less and less?

_____ 6. Is my conditioning about relationships or marriage affecting my decision to quit or stay?

_____ 7. Have I been denying any strong feelings which I might have about the relationship?

_____ 8. Is there little chance we can change things for the better?

_____ 9. Have I come to a point where there is no light at the end of the tunnel?

_____10. Has my situation eroded so slowly that I may not yet be aware how bad things really are?

_____11. Am I limiting myself by believing that there is just one person "meant to be" in my life?

Total _____ (R-1)

Might You Hurt Yourself If You Stay in This Relationship? (Chapter 5)

Place an X in the space next to questions you would answer yes. Record your answers and feelings in your log/journal.

_____ 1. Am I increasingly happy when I am by myself?

_____ 2. Could the price that this relationship demands be too high?

_____ 3. Have I been blocking what I really feel?

_____ 4. Am I afraid to communicate my feelings?

_____ 5. Do I have a hard time being myself when I'm with my partner?

_____ 6. Do I feel less good about myself when I'm around my partner?

_____ 7. Am I staying in this relationship just to protect my partner?

_____ 8. Is it possible that there is no hope for this relationship?

_____ 9. Is my partner expecting too much from me?

_____10. Am I staying in this relationship mainly because I have invested so much of my time and myself in it?

_____11. Is it likely that I have remained in this relationship mainly because I feared what others would think of me if I left it?

Total _____ (R-2)

Will Others Be Hurt If You Quit Your Relationship? (Chapter 6)

Place an X next to any question you answer yes. Write your feelings down in your log as you consider each of the questions.

_____ 1. Will my ending this relationship or marriage cause considerable inconvenience?

_____ 2. Is it possible that my partner might experience unusual emotional damage if I quit the relationship?

_____ 3. Could I be overrating my partner's capacity to make it on his/her own?

_____ 4. Will a quit significantly hurt my family?

_____ 5. Will a quit significantly hurt his/her family?

_____ 6. Would I leave *because* I want to hurt my partner?

_____ 7. Will my leaving cause any significant financial disruption for my partner?

_____ 8. Will my leaving cause unusual physical disruption (packing, moving, etc.) for my partner?

_____ 9. Will my leaving significantly disrupt any plans partner has?

Total _____ (R-3)

How Nourishing Is Your Relationship or Marriage? (Chapter 7)

As you look through the following questions, consider whether you are experiencing what is being described. If not, ask yourself if you think the two of you are capable of experiencing it. Boldly explore any feelings which surface as you consider these questions. Place an X next to each question you can honestly answer "yes."

_____ 1. Does your partner openly express appreciation for what you contribute to the relationship?

_____ 2. Are you told verbally that you are loved?

_____ 3. Do you sense that your partner enjoys being with you?

_____ 4. Do you basically feel good about being around your partner?

_____ 5. Does your partner convey the feeling that you are a positive influence in his or her life?

_____ 6. Do you feel there is a realistic balance between the efforts you are putting into the relationship and the rewards you are experiencing?

Total X's _____ (N-R)　　　　　　　　Total blanks _____ (R-4)

How Toxic Is Your Relationship?

As you read through the following questions, "listen" for any feelings which are aching to be heard. Place an X next to any question you answer "yes." Use your log!

_____ 1. Does your partner frequently criticize you?

_____ 2. Do you find more emphasis placed on your mistakes than your accomplishments?

_____ 3. Do you feel you have to make an excessive effort in order to get praise?

_____ 4. Does your partner frequently yell at you?

_____ 5. Does your partner criticize you in front of others?

_____ 6. Does your partner often lose his or her temper?

Total _____ (R-5)

References

Bolles, Richard Nelson, *What Color Is Your Parachute?* Berkeley, CA: Ten Speed Press, 1988 (Revised Annually)

Maltz, Maxwell, *Psycho-Cybernetics*. New York: Pocket Books (Other editions by Wilshire Book Company, Los Angeles, and Hazelden, Center City, Minnesota).